CHRISTIAN DISCOVERY

CHRISTIAN DISCOVERY

The Road to Justice

James J. DiGiacomo, S.J.
John J. Walsh, M.M.

ORBIS BOOKS
Maryknoll, New York 10545

The Catholic Foreign Mission Society of America (Maryknoll) recruits and trains people for missionary service. Through Orbis Books, Maryknoll aims to foster the international dialogue that is essential to mission. The books published, however, reflect the opinions of their authors and are not meant to represent the official position of the society.

Copyright © 1992 by James J. DiGiacomo and John J. Walsh
Published by Orbis Books, Maryknoll, New York 10545
Scripture citations are taken from *The New American Bible*, Revised Edition. Copyright © 1969, 1970, 1986, and 1990, Confraternity of Christian Doctrine.
Printed in the United States of America

Library of Congress Cataloging-in-Publication Data

DiGiacomo, James J., 1913-
   Christian discovery : the road to justice / James J. DiGiacomo, John J. Walsh.
     p. cm.
   Includes bibliographical references.
   ISBN 0-88344-807-6
   1. Christian life—Catholic authors. 2. Jesus Christ—Person and offices. I. Walsh, John J., 1913- . II. Title.
BX2350.2.D498   1992
248.4′82—dc20   91-41590
                                                        CIP

Contents

Introduction

As the twentieth century draws to a close, there is a feeling everywhere that something old is dying and something new is being born. The approach of a new century brings a sharpened sense of anticipation. How will our world be different? What opportunities and dangers await us as the Christian era enters its third millennium? How will *we* be different?

No doubt the world of politics and science and travel and medicine will be profoundly altered. And so will the world of religion, in ways less dramatic, perhaps, but no less significant. For it is to their religious beliefs that many have always looked to find meaning and stability in a changing world. It is religious faith that provides many of us with a sense of personal significance in the face of events and movements that might otherwise overwhelm us.

To those who want to make deeper sense of their lives, who seek resources for living that will survive whatever the future may bring, this book is addressed. In the new age that is coming, new perspectives and new opportunities for faith development confront us all. Many of us are seeking more mature insight into our personal religious journeys. We write in the conviction that the answers to our most perplexing questions and the fulfillment of our deepest longings are to be found in the Good News of Jesus Christ. But we also know that, though the Good News is always the same, the audience is constantly changing.

Alterations of the Christian consciousness have had an impact on our religious ideas, our points of view, and the way we express ourselves. Liberation theology, the quest for peace and justice outside and inside the church, the movement for women's rights, and the widening gulf between religious Americans and the culture of consumerism have all left their mark on us. One result of this religious ferment is this book, an attempt to relate the Gospel to our lives here and now. It is written with a diverse audience in mind. Catholics and other Christians will be most at home with the ideas and concerns expressed here. Older readers are invited to clarify and deepen their religious convictions in new and perhaps surprising ways. Younger adults will find much here for them as they seek solid grounding for their maturing religious identity as well as answers for questions that refuse to go away. Those who do not share the faith of the authors but find themselves in an open and inquiring stance may find enlightenment on their own road to faith. Those who have drifted away from church and religious practice are invited to take a second look at the altered terrain. There may even be a few older teenagers who are tired of religious kid food. They are invited to sneak under the tent and join the older folks, but are hereby warned that this is grown-up stuff.

The book is divided into three parts. Part one, Beginnings, explores the roots of religious experience and the genesis of faith. What are the questions that underlie our restlessness? Why is religion, as we have known it, so often disappointing? Who are the false gods who mock our aspirations? Will the real God please stand up?

Part two, Meetings, tells a story that we have heard before but perhaps never really listened to—the saga of Jesus Christ. The man, his message, and his deeds are portrayed in a new way, one calculated to get beneath the patina of fuzzy piety and help us encounter the challenging man beneath.

Part three, Gatherings, invites us to see what it means to throw in our lot with Christ in his Body, which is the church. A new church is struggling to come to birth, but it must first break out of obsolete, timid, self-serving patterns of behavior. A church as committed to justice as its founder is an ideal that faces formidable obstacles, but we should settle for nothing less.

The material in this book is suitable both for private reading and for group study. Adult education groups will find some excellent topics for discussion in the Things to Do section at the end of each chapter. Since readers are encouraged to go beyond the text and to integrate the ideas into their own life stories, this is probably the best way for most people to use this book. Whatever way is chosen, the authors hope and pray that it will be the occasion of many coming closer to Christ and to one another.

CHRISTIAN DISCOVERY

PART ONE

BEGINNINGS

1

Lonely in a Crowd

Have you ever felt lonely at a party?

Perhaps you remember that feeling and the thoughts that ran through your head. *We came here for a good time, but it's not happening. Something is missing. Maybe I shouldn't have come. Am I the only one who feels this way?*

Some of the guests are leaving early. Others are still here, but their hearts don't seem to be in it. Some are trying hard, talking but not being heard. Introverts are standing on the sidelines. Extroverts are talking but not listening. Some are jumping in, but in a lopsided way, eating too much or getting smashed.

What was the purpose of this party, anyway?

When a party turns out this way, the evening is a bummer. Too bad, but not tragic; you can't win them all. But what if this failed party seems to be a good description of your whole life? Sometimes we feel this way about ourselves. If it's more than a passing mood of depression, if it keeps coming back despite your attempts to keep busy or distract yourself, then it may be a sign that something is indeed missing from your life. This feeling may take many forms: a lack of communication, a lack of meaning, an experience of emptiness. Or a question: Is this all there is?

Several years ago a young woman named Caroline felt this way and wrote a very personal letter to the New York *Times* (November 12, 1967):

To The Editor:
    I am the wife of a promising young businessman, the

3

mother of two small boys, and I work at home as a free-lance copy editor. I have been out of Smith College almost five years. At 25, I am faced with the crisis of finding some meaning in life or, if that proves impossible, finding a satisfactory way of living and functioning despite it. . . .

The question is, how do you find something to look forward to? And how do you achieve that sense of purpose in what you are doing that will end this questioning? . . . I wonder how you go about feeling committed. What difference does it make whether I go back to school and get more educated or just read or go to painting classes or try to make a career out of something? Basically, what are goals of any kind in the face of death? Yet how is it possible to be happy in the present, forgetting goals, if there is no sense of accomplishing anything?

The trouble is that I, probably like many of the other alienated, can't get out of myself. I think mainly of me, and I am isolated in my thoughts. To be able to communicate in this impersonal way, that is, write a letter to the Times, is a pleasant relief, but still very self-orientated and of course very temporary.

What is the answer? Keep busier? See lots of people and communicate like mad? See a psychiatrist? Drugs?

Even more interesting than this letter is the way people react to it. Some say she's neurotic or unreasonable. After all, they reason, she has everything that most of us want but few of us have — family, money, education, security. She has no reason to feel so lonely at the party called life. But others identify with her and acknowledge that her complaints and questioning strike responsive chords within themselves. How about you? Can you identify with her in any way? Do her longings and questionings sound anything like yours?

Saint Augustine's explanation of this young woman's malaise is classic. He says our hearts are restless until they rest in God. Her letter is a primal cry for more, for some overarching meaning, for a sense of transcendent purpose. Facing her own mortality and the fragility of her hopes and dreams, she looks for some sense of enduring significance in her own life and in the world around her. Great philosophers have wrestled with her questions as they tried to figure out what life is all about. The world's religions are attempts to respond, not only with ideas, but with some formula for getting in touch with the infinite, with the mystery at the center of life.

A CRY FROM THE HEART

Caroline is asking religious questions. Not religious in the sense of "What church should I belong to?" but religious in a more fundamental sense. She is asking questions of ultimate meaning, the most basic queries we can put to life. And she is not just looking for the answer to a puzzle. More than curiosity is at work here. This is a cry from the heart, a search for Something or Someone that will fill the void in her life. The gigantic externalization of life in our culture tends to discourage such questions and stifle such longings, but they persist in rising to the surface every so often and plaguing us with a sense of our incompleteness.

Saint Augustine would say that—whether she knows it or not—Caroline is looking for God. And perhaps you perceived at first glance that the answer to her question lay in some kind of religious faith. You were right, but we should beware of giving her too facile an answer. If she struck a chord only in the hearts of unbelievers, that would be one thing. But the fact is that some devoutly religious people have much the same experience, and this is even more disturbing to them. When people who think of themselves as Christians find that they, too, are lonely at the party called life, they wonder about the quality of their faith and the reality of its object. They are surprised that they, too, are subject to feelings of alienation from God and others, even from themselves. Religion is supposed to fulfill our deepest personal needs, yet often doesn't. Why?

When we experience thoughts and feelings like those of Caroline, we may be moved to ask, as she does: What should I do? This book is an attempt to answer that question. We believe that there is a way out of meaninglessness and despair, that religious faith offers not a dispensation from life's pain and struggle but a satisfying answer to our deepest questioning and the fulfillment of the most profound desires of our hearts. In describing that way we shall be like physicians prescribing medicine and treatment. But, as any good doctor will tell you, effective prescription depends on accurate diagnosis, so let us spend a little time analyzing how we came to this present crisis. Why do feelings of emptiness and futility afflict not only those who lack faith or are seeking it, but even many of those who thought they had found it? Why does this cosmic loneliness show up not only among those outside the church or on its fringe, but even inside, indeed in the very sanctuary?

One may well wonder if such a diagnosis is possible in these pages. Aren't we all unique? Isn't each person's experience so personal as to defy generalization? Moreover, the people who read this book will probably be situated across a broad spectrum of attitudes, from skepticism and apathy at one end to belief and commitment at the other, with all kinds of variations in between. Amid such diversity, is it possible to find any common threads? We think it is. Although each of us is unique, it is still true that we share a world and many experiences. Certain events and movements in the church and in the wider world have had an impact on us all, on our capacity to believe in ourselves, to reach out to others, and to search for and open ourselves to God.

HOW WE GOT THIS WAY

Some people try to make sense of their lives and derive satisfaction from them in nonreligious ways. There are many reasons for this. They may seek personal wholeness in the ways offered by the dominant culture of consumerism: through possessions, pleasure, power, and prestige. Believing the powerful message of advertising that says products can fulfill our deepest needs, they give themselves completely to the pursuit of money and the things money can buy, hopeful that affluence can heal all ills and satisfy all desires. When they find out that these promises are empty, the result is a disillusionment that can be shattering and lead either to despair or to a hope for something better. Caroline may possibly be such a person, and her letter may reflect this kind of crisis.

When people perceive the spiritual bankruptcy of consumerism, they may look for an alternative way of life. But religion, far from attracting them, may repel them. The churchy squabbles, the hypocrisy of some religious leaders, the mediocrity and parochialism of rank-and-file church members turn them off. To them it seems that institutional religion, far from shedding light, provides only gratuitous complication. Instead of enriching its devotees, it seems to impoverish them, to make them less human. And so they look for meaning in some form of humanism, in frantic activities, in trendy self-help formulas promising psychic wholeness, or in some vague form of individualistic idealism.

The authors of *Habits of the Heart* tell us of Sheila Larson, a young nurse who has actually named her religion after herself: "I believe in God. I'm not a religious fanatic. I can't remember the last time I went to church. My faith has carried me a long way. It's Sheilaism. Just my own little voice." In defining "my own Sheilaism," she said, "It's just try to love yourself and be gentle with yourself. You know, I guess, take care of each other. I think He would want us to take care of one another" (p. 221).

Only when people learn from personal experience how limited these strategies are, will they be possibly open to mainline religious affiliation and involvement.

There are those within the fold who thought that church membership and fidelity to its rules and practices would exempt them from the thousand natural shocks that unbelievers are heir to. But while their religion provides them with valued resources for dealing with life's sternest challenges, it has also involved them in a bewildering series of developments that leave them alternately enlightened and confused, enthusiastic and discouraged, contented and angry, united and polarized. It is time to look at some of these events that have left Christians feeling lonely at their own party, alienated from members of their own household, and looking for a way to fill the void in their lives that they know should not be there.

The last third of the twentieth century has been a time of extraordinary turmoil in the life of the church. The pace of change and the sheer volume of alterations, not only in church style and practice, but even in the way people think of themselves as Christian, have been breathtaking. Even the most optimistic members of the post-Vatican II church must admit that a heavy price has been paid for the process of renewal. For example, the rites of celebration of the Eucharist and Reconciliation have been much improved, but these sacraments are neglected by great numbers of the faithful. Religious education theory and practice have been greatly refined, but many still suffer from religious illiteracy. Large investments of talent and energy have gone into youth ministry, yet distressingly large numbers of young people have been lost to the Christian community. New forms of adult ministry such as cursillo, marriage encounter, and charismatic prayer groups have enriched the church, but the loss of old symbols and devotions has left many feeling adrift.

The coming of age of the laity in sharing responsibility for the life of the church has not completely made up for the severe drop in the number of vocations to the priesthood and religious life. The wounds left by the birth control controversy have not all healed, and the crisis of authority and obedience remains unresolved and lurking just beneath the surface. The alienation of so many women who feel oppressed and unappreciated within present church structure is a source of real pain in the Body of Christ. Many of those who remember the monolithic, undisturbed unity of the American church at midcentury still feel disoriented and see a church that has lost much of its vitality and its ability to fire the imagination and enlist the loyalty of the faithful. Even those who feel at home in the postconciliar era are saddened by the losses incurred in the attempt to adapt to a changing world. Finally, there is a third group of church members who go along with contemporary policies but without enthusiasm, harking back to a past that seemed better but cannot be reclaimed.

This brief and by no means complete survey of the dislocations that have occurred in church life in recent years goes far toward explaining the malaise that afflicts the Christian family. But this diagnosis of the ills that beset us will be incomplete if we do not try to understand better why the road to church renewal has been such a rocky one. We do not adequately account for the divisions among and within people by simply pointing to the phenomena of pluralism and division. We must go deeper and ask why people react so differently to religious realities. What are the sources of the divisions among and within us?

The beginning of understanding lies in recognizing the fact that people appropriate or take possession of the faith in three very distinct ways. These kinds of faith appropriation influence the way they interpret their beliefs and try to act on them. Some people know only one way throughout their lives, others progress from one to another. These passages, when they occur, can change many aspects of their lives, not just the religious. We call these three ways of appropriating religious values *traditional, transitional,* and *integrated.*

TRADITIONAL FAITH

All of us, when we were children, received from our parents and other significant adults some form of faith. The word *faith* is used here in the broadest sense, as any kind of belief system, whether Christianity or some other religion or even atheism or agnosticism. James Fowler calls this faith a way of perceiving our ultimate environment. This worldview was accepted uncritically, by a process loosely described as indoctrination. We were then socialized into this faith as we grew up and learned to follow its teachings in a nonjudgmental way. Various elements and institutions supported and affirmed us in this way of looking at life — school, neighborhood, church community.

From our earliest beginnings, this shared faith gave us a sense of being united with others who were like us. This experience of union was achieved by uniformity of belief and behavior. It is a lot like joining a parade: keeping in step, following directions, accepting without question both the goals of the group and the approved means of achieving them. At this precritical level we attain community by repressing individuality. Criticism is equated with disloyalty. Questioning sounds like rebellion. Individuality is confused with individualism. Taking responsibility for one's own ideas and actions seems like nothing less than betrayal, for parades function best when all march to the same drummer, resist any impulse to nonconformity, and walk neither faster nor more slowly than anyone else.

All armies, most companies, many organizations, and some churches prefer to operate in this fashion. Their members achieve such goals as idealism, community, and a sense of belonging by submerging their individuality and blending in with the group. From this uncritical adherence to communal ideals and discipline they may draw the strength needed for commitment, sacrifice, even heroism. They are the true believers who can be counted on in a crisis, who can submerge their doubts in a single-minded dedication to a cause or an institution. It must be noted, however, that though this level of faith appropriation can release and support great energy, it is passive in origin. It comes not from within the person but from without. In its beginnings it is imposed by elders or other authority figures whose legitimacy and competence are unquestioned. As long as it is accepted and left unchallenged, it can be a source of great strength.

Some of these true believers spend their whole lives at this traditional faith level. At their best they have a sense of wholeness, a clear vision of reality, and an identity rooted in a group consensus. At their worst they may be rigid, narrow, intolerant, and subject to manipulation. In short, they have purchased some very desirable qualities, but at a price. When this price is perceived as too high, when the limitations of traditional faith appropriation become unacceptable, the person may make the move to transitional faith.

TRANSITIONAL FAITH

This second level of faith appropriation takes many forms, but certain characteristics are common to all. Whether or not we clearly perceive what is going on, we are being moved to own our faith not from the outside but from the inside. We experience a deep psychological need to reexamine our beliefs and commitments and submit them to a more searching appraisal. Something is going on here that resembles what a convert goes through in moving from one church to another. Old certainties lack their power to convince. Previously unchallenged authorities look vulnerable. Repressed doubts rise to the surface. As the ruler in *The King and I* sings, "There are times I am not sure of what I absolutely know." And there begins an internal, inside-out, active effort to take possession of our faith-life values.

A young man, the student of one of the authors, vividly described this experience, which he saw going on in himself and among his peers:

> The youth of today are more independent, more self-reliant than ever before. They question everything they meet. They are less willing to accept doctrines and judgments as being right without first examining them and judging them on personal experience. This type of "skepticism" concerning that which presently exists extends to the belief in God and worship of Him through religion. Young people are no longer content to accept the religion of their parents and teachers as being the one of truth simply because it is the religion of these people and the religion they are taught when young. Instead of quiet acceptance, there is common in youth today, more than ever before, a point or period of crisis during which the individual realizes he must choose either to accept or to reject the faith before him. The consequences of this decision are so great that, I believe, many young people do not really make a definite choice without hesitation or doubt for several years.

This agonizing reappraisal can be disquieting, guilt ridden, confusing, exciting, and exhilarating all at once. Antoine Vergote, a religious psychologist, calls it the crisis of adult faith and describes it as a movement from obedience, dependence, submission, and docility to initiative, independence, creativity, and healthy skepticism. It often involves a sense of discontinuity and rupture, a feeling that old boundaries and guideposts are no longer in force. When this happens, the old faith may simply be rejected, to be replaced by uprootedness and anomie. On the other hand, there may be instead a sense of enrichment, an opening up of larger possibilities and better things, a sense of growth and positive challenge.

Even this more positive form of transition, however, is characterized by a certain one-sidedness, a lack of balance. One may insist on logical consistency or rigorous intellectual honesty while neglecting the affective dimension of religious experience. Such a person stresses the role of the head at the expense of the heart. Conversely, another may concentrate on feeling to the exclusion of intellect. Then there are those who put so much emphasis on individual authenticity that they ignore the demands of community. In the opposite vein, their counterparts seek community without a corresponding respect for individuality. Some cultivate prayer and the spiritual life and lose all interest in active service of the neighbor, while others fall into the opposite error of activism devoid of nourishing interiority.

Notice that in each of these cases transitional persons seek a positive good, fastening on some genuine aspect of faith. Their only fault is in neglecting another good at the opposite pole. At this stage they tend to be judgmental, undervaluing faith expressions different from their own but deserving of respect, and are prone to elitism and polarization. These are normal growing pains for persons who have begun to take responsibility for their own existence, and are not too great a problem as long as the transitional phase is truly transitional and not terminal. Ideally, the person should move on to a further phase of appropriation, that of integrated faith.

INTEGRATED FAITH

The person who moves from passive to active appropriation of faith and from unquestioning acceptance to reflective commitment faces the further challenge of dealing with dialectic and paradox. A higher level of maturity is needed to hold in creative tension such polarities as heart and head, individuality and community, action and contemplation, obedience and creativity, compromise and integrity. The integrated, mature person is one capable not only of taking personal responsibility but also of reconciling and peacemaking. A new balance has been struck, a fresh serenity has been achieved. This is not a lukewarm middle-of-the-roader who strives for peace at any price but a truly liberated person who can appreciate a variety of gifts and bring people together. Unfortunately, such people are in rather short supply.

There may have been a time, not long ago, when traditional faith was enough to keep Christians marching together and serving the faith community. But a number of recent historical developments have conspired to produce large numbers of people of transitional faith and to create a pressing need for persons of integrated faith who will keep the community from coming apart. The Nuremberg trials at the end of World War II exposed the inadequacy of unquestioning loyalty and obedience to one's government and military superiors. The Vietnam War and the civil rights struggles of the sixties forced people to think in new ways about just and unjust laws, about civil disobedience, and about the limits of loyalty. The birth control controversy precipitated a crisis of conscience within the Catholic Church that is still with us. The movement for women's rights continues to disturb and divide us as a nation and as a church. These and other controversies and struggles have done away with national and religious consensus and have shattered forever the image of a monolithic church. Unity by uniformity is now only a fading memory, and it is not yet clear what has taken its place. It is no wonder that so many of us are disoriented, feeling like strangers in our own house, lonely at a party that was supposed to be a celebration.

This, in brief, is our diagnosis of the crisis that confronts us as individuals and as a community of faith. We tend to think of a crisis as a bad thing, a time of trouble, a period of danger. But the word indicates rather a turning point, a dangerous moment fraught with possibilities both good and bad. The outcome will depend not only on God's action but on our response. How should we respond to this critical moment? Life and death have been set before us. It is time to prescribe a course of action whereby, in the fullest sense, we may choose not death but life.

Things to Do

1. The first practical, concrete thing you can do is start a journal. This is your own private record of your thoughts, feelings,

and experiences. If you are part of a group, you may sometimes choose to share some of your reflections.

2. Three persons are quoted at some length—Caroline, Sheila,
   and the young student. Did any of them strike a responsive
   chord in you? Did you see something of yourself in any of
   them?

3. How do you react to Caroline? Does she evoke in you feelings
   of sympathy, impatience, or something else? Can you identify
   with her at all? If you could speak to her, what would you
   say?

4. Have you ever felt about God or religion or church the way
   Sheila does? If you could speak to her, what would you say?

5. Does the young student's expression of hesitation and doubt
   resemble any experiences you have ever had? If you could
   speak to him, what would you say?

2

Don't Just Sit There

All living is meeting.
—Martin Buber

The reader never gets to see some of the most important characters in the *Peanuts* comic strip. One of these is the little redheaded girl in Charlie Brown's school. For years he tried to get up courage to cross the schoolyard and introduce himself, but couldn't. The problem was not with the girl, of course, but with Charlie. Full of hang-ups, burdened with a negative self-image, he couldn't take the initiative in an encounter with another human being. If he could just break the ice, maybe the two of them might become good friends. He kept hoping that it would happen to him in spite of his doing nothing. Afraid to risk rejection and failure, he took refuge in daydreams.

Did you ever return, as an adult, to the schoolyard where you played as a child? Did you notice how small it had become? The yard that looked so big to Charlie Brown was really very small. The distance and the difficulty were all in his own mind. So is the distance between us and others, between us and God.

The Japanese have an interesting and perceptive word for encounter: *deai. De* means "to go out of," and *ai* means "to meet." You must go out before you can meet. We know from experience that we must go out of ourselves in order to meet the other, whether that other is God or another human being. There is a leap involved here, and it is sometimes scary—so scary that some people spend their lives avoiding the risk. They have

15

associates, colleagues, acquaintances—but no friends. Others become experts on religion—scripture scholars, sociologists or psychologists of religion, even theologians—but have no faith. For them, the problem of relationships or of religion is just that: a problem, a puzzle. They get no closer to other people or to God than Charlie Brown gets to the redheaded girl.

Most people divide their lives into compartments: work, play, sleep, travel. Each has its assigned percentage of life. If religion gets a share, it's usually just a few percent and assigned to the ornament class—nice to have, but not essential. Religion comes in handy at weddings and funerals, but most people don't lose sleep over it. One way to break out of this sterile pattern is to step back and take a fresh look at our lives.

Look at your life: work, play, sleep, travel. Every day is made up of experiences that are good or bad, neutral, boring, hopeful. As you try to locate yourself in these experiences, you find that they are bigger than you, in the sense that you cannot explain them solely in terms of yourself. You cannot express what life is about unless you go beyond yourself. You cannot find the full meaning of any experience or event in your life until you extend it to include both yourself and the other.

Consider your life up to now. Pick out the three or four greatest happinesses in your life. If you examine them carefully, you'll find that for the most part they involved other people. Any experience in your life takes on full meaning only when it's done with someone or is shared in some way with someone. There is a meeting with someone, whether other people or God. This meeting or encounter with God and others is what we call religion. From this point of view, religion is the most natural, the most ordinary thing in the world. When we see religion as encounter, then life and religion are one and the same.

All day long the opportunity to encounter presents itself. You find yourself with people, so there's a chance to encounter them. Of course, there's more to encountering than just being with them, but the opportunity is there. There's nothing in your life that God isn't interested in. Not just the dramatic things, but also the humdrum, prosaic things. God even finds you interesting. Suddenly life and religion are one.

As long as you see Christianity only as a system, an ethic, a philosophy—something to be studied the way you studied subjects at school—nothing important happens. You may learn a lot about religion, but you'll never have faith. You may even learn something *about* God, but you won't *know* God. Even after you get your doctorate in theology and publish your tenth book on religion, you'll be an outsider, like Charlie Brown. It works the same way for scholars and mechanics, senior citizens and teenagers: You must take the risk, go out of yourself, and encounter God and others.

There will be a place for study afterwards. When people fall in love, they want to know more and more about each other: where they come from, where they live, their work, their interests, tastes, ideas. When God becomes real and important to us, we want to know what God is really like, and study can help. But that's later, after you cross the schoolyard and introduce yourself. Come on, Charlie Brown, don't be wishy-washy.

The language we use to describe religious experience sometimes obscures the reality. We use expressions such as "She has a deep faith," "He's very religious," "He prays a lot," "She's devoted to the church." The language is misleading because it gives the impression that religious experience centers about some *thing.* That faith or church or prayer just happens to be some people's "thing." True, there are people who use religion this way, but authentic religious experience isn't like that. It's not about something, but about Someone. Human beings are caught up with a Reality infinitely greater than themselves—a Reality that's present in a mysterious way, a Reality that's personal. No word is adequate to express this Reality, but we have to use some word, and in our language and culture that word is God.

Some people say that this God is not really personal but is just some force, feeling, or energy at the heart of the universe. Still others say God is just a name for the love between people or for the best instincts of humankind. But Christians insist that God is personal, knows us by name, cares for us, speaks to us, listens to us. For serious Christians, religion and prayer and faith and church are not values in themselves, but they have great value because they are ways of being in touch with God.

Religion is the attempt to relate to a personal God, to know and love One who knows and loves me first. Faith is more than an optimistic way of looking at the world; it's an abiding trust in a God who is faithful. Prayer is dialogue—sometimes speaking, sometimes listening, sometimes doing nothing but being with God—and a church is ideally a community that shares a faith and strives for union with God.

As you can see, in all this we are simply describing a relationship between persons. It's a very special one, to be sure, because one of the terms of the relationship is God. But, special as it is, it's still subject to the laws that govern all interpersonal relationships. So if you want to know how a person can relate to God, you must first reflect on how you relate to other human beings. Consider in particular the relationship of friendship.

How do you get to be friends with another person? It can happen in a thousand different ways. Two people meet at a party and hit it off. Fellow workers find they have something in common besides a job and skills and deadlines. A man and a woman meet at a dance or at a bar or at work and find they enjoy each other's company. Sometimes people start out disliking each other, but some shared experience turns things around and makes them friends. Most of these friendships aren't very deep or permanent. They fail to survive the end of a vacation, graduation, or a change of job or address. Others go much deeper and endure for many years, even for a lifetime. Some are formalized in marriage, where two become one and share their whole lives in bonds of closest intimacy.

All friendships, the brief and the lasting, the shallow and the deep, follow certain observable patterns. They begin with encounter, and they are nourished by dialogue, by sharing, and even by total self-giving, or they dwindle and fade because those things are lacking.

Before you can become someone's friend, you must encounter that person. Think of all the people who have crossed your path. Some you got to know. About others, you never cared one way or the other. If you became friends with someone, it was by sharing something—asking for help, enjoying a laugh together, working together on a project. You shared your feelings, your time, your opinions. You did things together after work or on weekends. When that happens you have a friend, maybe even a close friend. The other people you see every day are just there; this one is *with* you. When you need help, she's the one you turn to. She's the first one you tell good news to. There are secrets you share with no one else. This is the stuff of friendship, and it starts when two people notice each other, let down their defenses, and begin to build a relationship.

That's how we meet our friends, and that's how we meet God, too.

For some of our readers, this makes perfect sense, because they already know it from experience. To them, God has always been real, always present, interested in them and attentive to them. But for others, there may be problems. Maybe they've always believed in God, but not a God to whom they could relate in such a personal way. A creator or a lawgiver or a rewarder or a punisher, maybe, but not a close friend. Some may even be wondering at this point about the very existence of God. How can someone fill a void in your life when you're not even sure that someone is real?

These are genuine difficulties that must be taken seriously. Just from the way they are expressed, we can tell that the usual problem-solving techniques won't work here. Trying to figure out whether God exists and what God is like are fascinating intellectual exercises, but they are not the answer. We don't just want to know *about* God; we want to *know* God. We're looking not for ideas but for an experience. But how can you make that experience happen?

Well, you can't, for the same reason that you can't force any friendship to happen. There are no recipes or prepackaged formulas for relationships. Like people whom we just casually knew before becoming friends, God is always there, never forcing the issue but waiting for us to notice and respond. God is always with us, whether we respond or not. We don't even have to take the initiative. In fact, we don't have to *do* anything! All that is needed is to make a little time or space to open ourselves up to the Other who is already reaching out to us. In the words of the old Beatles song, "Let it be."

This attentiveness to the Other, this willingness to let go and accept an invitation from God, is really a type of prayer. Before any words are said, just by listening or being in another's pres-

ence, something important is happening between you. Just by
being willing to share and receive, you have taken a leap out of
yourself. This is the *de* that must happen before there can be
an *ai* — a meeting, an encounter. The ball is now in God's court;
wait and see what happens.

Sometimes it may be a good while before anything seems to
happen. In most religious activities we like to see results right
away. We tend to judge a homily or a liturgy or a retreat by
whether it issues in immediate enthusiasm or action. But here
we are talking rather about a kind of time-bomb effect, where
something is happening below the threshold of consciousness
and will become evident only later on. As in any evolutionary
process, progress is much slower and less obvious at the initial
stages. Buildings go up much faster at the end than at the beginning.

Sometimes there is genuine spiritual progress, but we may
underrate our development because we are unable to articulate
the experience. Or we may reach a critical point early in the
process and spend time wrestling with a difficult point of acceptance. However, once the critical point is passed, progress is
often very rapid. Anxiety and frustration will be reduced if we
entertain realistic expectations.

In reaching out to God and others, don't look for instant
progress. This is a long-haul project. With the shift from external
to internal appropriation of faith, the results are usually not
immediate, but they go deeper and last longer. Sometimes we
are genuinely changed for the better by the gospel message we
hear, but the change is not perceptible right away.

We may come out of a prayer group, liturgical celebration,
or retreat and feel that nothing significant has happened. Ask
us at that moment what we got out of it, and in all honesty the
answer is "nothing." We don't *feel* any different, so we presume
we aren't any different. But a few days or a week or even much
later, we have an experience that surprises us. Perhaps in meeting a challenge we show unaccustomed courage. A cross is laid
on us, and we are surprised at our ability to carry it. An unfore-
seen opportunity to serve may come our way, and we respond
with a generosity we didn't know we had. What we didn't know
was that an encounter time bomb was ticking in our heart, and

only now does the actual love encounter take place. The timing of such encounters, of course, depends not only on the human spirit but on the Holy Spirit.

Encounters may not be immediate, and they cannot be programmed, but when they do come, they are powerful and long-lived. This book itself may be an occasion for such time bombs. They may be intellectual, leading to deeper insights into our faith, or more importantly, they may be encounter time bombs leading to new and deeper meetings with God and others.

"Well, all right," you say, "I'll try to pray. But how?"

1. Pray in your own words, if you want. Tell God what's in your heart and on your mind, right at this moment. Don't make your language too formal. It's hard to develop a friendship when people are stiff and formal with each other.

2. You don't have to use words at all, if you don't want to. Think *together with* God about your life. That's praying.

3. Imagine yourself on a hike with a friend. In the beginning it's "yak, yak, yak." As you go along, though, and begin to climb mountains, the words become fewer and fewer. Finally the two of you arrive out of breath at the top. A magnificent scene lies at your feet. No words are spoken. Who needs them? Encounter without words.

4. Try to be aware, if only for a moment, that God is with you and finds you interesting. On a train, while walking, at the factory or office, having a drink, resting, watching TV—anytime at all. When you do that, the train, the walk, the rest all become prayer.

5. Open a Bible and read slowly and reflectively. Not all parts of the Bible are appropriate, but many are. In the New Testament, the words and deeds of Christ can be thought provoking and inspirational. In the Old Testament, the Psalms are prayers you can say yourself. These are poems and songs that people have used for over 2,500 years in meeting God. They express universal experiences and emotions such as sadness, thanksgiving, loneliness, cries for help. You can find one to fit any mood or situation.

These are just some of the ways you might try to pray. Choose ways you feel comfortable with. Prayer may come much more easily than you think. Even if it doesn't—if you find stubborn resistance or inertia within yourself or if you feel that you're speaking into a void—don't give up too easily. Some of the most valuable things in our lives don't come easily at first.

If Charlie Brown ever gets up enough courage to cross the schoolyard and introduce himself to the little redheaded girl, he may feel as if he has finally arrived. If the two of them become friends, he may think that he has finally found the one he's been looking for. Of course, what he doesn't know is that this isn't the end, but only the beginning of a fascinating journey. By doing *deai*, going out of himself and encountering the other, he has unlocked possibilities in both of them. What begins as an acquaintance could develop into a friendship, maybe even into a deep and lasting love. Their relationship may be a smooth and serene one, or their path could be strewn with misunderstanding as well as comprehension, quarrels as well as closeness, pain as well as joy. But the important thing is that he has begun. Because he took a chance and made himself vulnerable, new possibilities have opened up that were closed to him as long as he remained alone.

When we feel dissatisfied or disappointed with our lives, lonely at the party called life, wondering if this is all there is, we may be at a critical point rich in opportunity. Now we are on the threshold of becoming searching persons. Like Caroline, who failed to find contentment in the midst of affluence and security, we are experiencing the first stirrings of a quest for the infinite. We can repress the longing, quiet the feelings of dissatisfaction, and take refuge in the familiar. Or we can take the risk, expose ourselves to the possibility of rejection and disappointment, and set forth into the unknown, where the object of our longing awaits and invites us.

Things to Do

1. What is the point of the Charlie Brown story? What does it have to do with religion?
2. The basic theme of this chapter can be expressed in the following equation: Religion = Encounter = Life. Explain this in your own words.

3. "Religion is not about some*thing* but about Someone." Explain.
4. What is the difference between knowing about God and knowing God?
5. From your own life, give the case history of a friendship. How did it start? How did it develop? Is it still going on, or is it a thing of the past? What made these things happen?
6. Make one or more suggested attempts at prayer. Write in your journal how it went. Feel free to share all or part or none of it with the others in the group.

3

Breaking Out

Question: How many psychiatrists does it take to
change a light bulb?
Answer: One. But the light bulb has to *want* to
change.

The search for God and others usually begins with a cry,
explicit or implicit, for meaning. We all yearn for a sense of
significance. We want to believe that we make a difference, that
our lives count for something. When that sense of significance
is eroded or lost, we reach a crisis. Maybe possessions, pleasure,
power, and prestige have failed to satisfy us the way we
expected, and now we wonder how to nourish the spiritual part
of ourselves. Or perhaps religion and religious routines have
grown stale, and we either abandon them or look for ways to
infuse new life into them. When the old arguments no longer
convince and the old certainties start slipping away, we look for
firmer ground on which to stand. Overcoming our inertia is difficult, though, and the first step on the journey is usually the
longest and most arduous. But with that step we become searching persons. Now that we have emerged from our rut, something
can happen.

How can you carry on this search? How can you take that
first step? In a few moments we will offer some concrete suggestions. But first, remember what we said earlier about traditional, transitional, and integrated faith. Faith, as the term is
used here, is not some particular religion but a way of looking

at life that may or may not be conventionally religious. If up to now you have been at the stage called traditional faith, where your beliefs and values have been formed by uncritical adherence to group norms and traditions, your present impulse to search may come from a felt need to interiorize them in a more individual, active way. If you have been at the stage called transitional faith, that disquieting, exhilarating passage from passive to autonomous appropriation, you may now be experiencing a call to integrated faith, with its more nuanced response to dialectic and paradox. Depending on what stage you are at—and it is not always easy to know this about ourselves—certain features of your search will vary. But it is our conviction that, regardless of what stage you may be coming from, the movement toward wholeness is fundamentally the same.

You cannot, all by yourself, live the meaningful life you long for. Neither can you evolve into the interesting person you were meant to be. For these things to happen, you must get together with God and other people. But this cannot happen unless you want it to, for you are free.

One of the most marvelous things about any person is freedom. If a puppy dog comes up to you wagging his tail and nuzzling your hand, that's nice. But you know that if your hand goes away, he'll quickly go and find another one, for you realize that he came to you not by choice but by instinct.

If, on the other hand, a human being comes to you and says, with or without words, "I want to be your friend" or "I love you!" this really turns you on. Why? Because this person freely chose you and went out of his or her way to pick you. Wow! Likewise, you are free to respond or to hold back, to take a chance on growth or to play it safe and stay right where you are.

How can you stop playing it safe and take a chance? If you have reached the point where you can ask that question and really want an answer, then it's time to stop talking and act. Here are three things to do. The first two you should do right now, before you read or discuss any more. The third one will take longer, but now's the time to start.

PROJECT ONE

Do a review of your life up till now. What we're asking you to do here is to step back and get an overview of your life as a whole. What do you think of it, up to now? There are some things you had no control over: where you were born, rich or poor, short or tall. For the rest, try for a balanced view — not too easy, not too strict; not too optimistic, not too pessimistic. Strive for reality.

If you find it hard to get started, here are some suggestions:

• People in your life. Who played leading roles in your life? How? Did you play a part in others' lives?

• Things you've done. Accomplishments, disappointments, a high point, a low point.

• Places you've been. Where you've lived, where you just touched base or passed through. Did they make a difference?

• Turning points. Any pivotal events that set or changed the direction of your life. Or has it been pretty much a straight line?

• Goals, values, hopes, fears, ideals. What are the things that have moved you or stopped you or turned you aside? What have you been seeking or running from? What has made you tick?

PROJECT TWO

Spell out what you want to happen in life. Here we want you to pull out the stops. Think big! Tell yourself what you really want to happen in your life. Most of us are small-time operators, afraid to aim high lest we fall short, afraid to ask for too much lest we be disappointed. We brag about how no one or nothing is going to fence us in, and then we spend most of our time fencing ourselves in.

Many people have a tunnel vision of their future. They have a very limited, narrow view of what they want out of existence. What they want from life is mostly just what they can attain by themselves, so their future is mostly a tunnel they walk alone.

In this state of mind, we're not open to most religious messages. But if we break out of this cramped and cramping perspective and expand our heart wishes, what happens? We realize that we cannot attain these expanded heart wishes by ourselves. We see that to make them even begin to come true, we have to encounter God and others. This is where we get our working description of religion: Religion = Encountering God and Others.

So think big. Let yourself go. Don't be afraid to dream. What do you want to happen from here on in? Get beyond generalities. Spell out at least one concrete heart wish. What is it? Can you attain it all by yourself?

A word of warning. Some people are really great at this project. They have wonderful aspirations, really care for others, honestly want to do some great things, and have a tremendous capacity for love. When it comes to doing something to bring all this about, and the action is ordinary, fine, no problem. But if it involves a real sacrifice, a real change, a real leap out of oneself to the other, then nothing happens.

PROJECT THREE

Start to make it happen. As you did Project Two, you may have noticed certain patterns. When you analyze your desires and goals and hopes and dreams, no matter how varied they are, you find that certain basic desires emerge. If they did, it's because God put them in your heart. Among them are probably these:

• You want to love.
• You want to be loved.
• You want to encounter, to share with others.
• You want to blossom out, to realize all your potentialities to the full.

Love is an overworked and abused word that defies precise definition, but let's at least try to describe it. When I truly love others, I have more than a warm feeling toward them. To some extent I go out of myself and want to make them happy. If I succeed, my own happiness is thereby increased. When I love others this way, I share not only joy but also sorrow, hurt, and loneliness. If those I love are hurting, I try to remove or diminish their pain. Failing that, I want at least to share it, to assure them that they are not alone and that we are in this together.

Not only joys and sorrows are transformed by this reaching out to the beloved. Even the prosaic, humdrum experiences of life take on a special quality when done together. And when my love is returned, my own joys and sorrows and ordinary experiences come alive in a special way. This love attains its possibilities when it goes beyond individual relationships and enlarges its scope to take in others in the community. When two people really care for each other, their love spills over into ever-widening circles in an expanding world.

To share means to be in solidarity with others. I want to have a part in the experiences and feelings of others, and I want them to take part in mine. When we analyze many of our hearts' fondest desires, this feature appears over and over again. The things that mean the most to us are things that we do not want to keep to ourselves, so we not only share them with immediate friends but gradually enter into an ever-widening solidarity with the world—especially with those most in need of justice.

When we say we want to blossom out, we recognize that there are untapped reservoirs of talent and ability within us, waiting to come to the surface. This longing for realization and fulfillment finds its noblest expression when we want to realize our capacities together with others—not only with friends and acquaintances, but in an ever-widening community where people treat one another with justice and compassion. We cannot feel fulfilled as long as there are people in the world who are stunted and diminished and prevented from blossoming out themselves.

Concretely, how you want these things to happen may differ from what the next person wants, but when you let yourself dream big, these desires are going to appear.

Now it's time to get down to business, to get ready to receive the fulfillment of your hopes and dreams. That can happen, if you avoid falling into either of two traps.

The first trap is to become a dynamic nondoer. The dynamic nondoer is long on talk, tops on theory, great on plans and dreams, but short on action, real openness, and real ability to change and do.

The other trap you can fall into is to become a hundred-percenter. If the hundred-percenter can't attain 100 percent of all the desires uncovered in Project Two, then he or she wants out. Such people resign from life: If they can't excel 100 percent, then they're going to excel zero percent. The name of the game, ladies and gentlemen, is that you may have to settle for a lot less than 100 percent in this phase of your life. That's the bad news. The good news is that the batter who hits .333 may be put out twice as often as he hits safely, but he is still considered a star.

Why did we urge you to think big and expand your heart wishes? Were we putting you on? No. You must understand that it is God who put those desires in your heart and who will fulfill them—not on your schedule, but in God's good time. You're not going to do it all by yourself. Nothing is going to happen until you get together with God and other people, which is nothing more or less than our definition of religion.

This definition is quite different from the one that most people think of when they hear the word *religion*. Ask people on the street what it means, and most of their answers will come down to some variation of this: Religion is adhering to the sacred customs of one's group. Break it down and it includes beliefs, rituals, and moral prescriptions. This is all right as far as it goes, but it doesn't go far enough. It doesn't deny but seems to ignore the role of interpersonal relationships among ourselves and God and one another. As we pointed out earlier, it seems to be about things rather than persons.

Another more serious problem with the conventional understanding of religion is that it no longer motivates people the way it once did. There was a time when Christianity operated quite well at the traditional level of faith appropriation. At this level a church or religious community resembles a parade in which members march together in uncritical obedience to rules laid down by an unquestioned authority. When religion is "done" this way, it meets our needs for stability and a sense of belonging but neglects individuality and critical thinking. As people move from traditional to transitional levels of faith appropriation, the parade metaphor no longer satisfies. They feel the need to take responsibility for themselves, their beliefs, and their commitments. Unquestioning loyalty no longer satisfies them as a model of religious experience.

At this point a person may be tempted to jettison religion altogether. An alternative would be to settle for a kind of religious consumerism. Here a church is valued simply as a handy vehicle for such events as christenings, weddings, and funerals. These tribalistic rituals have no real impact on one's values, commitments, or one's way of life. This does not mean that we are talking about a bad person but about someone for whom religion is not much more than a piece of costume jewelry to be worn only on special occasions. A third possibility is to be religious in a new way: examining beliefs, weighing evidence, thinking critically, preserving one's individuality. This is what we call the transitional level of faith appropriation.

The question of preserving individuality is at the heart of many a crisis of faith and is worth dwelling on a bit longer. This book is about finding God and other people and letting them into our lives. Other people, at least in theory, are not a problem. Even those of us who are not very good at relating to others are intellectually convinced that meaningful human relationships are an important part of any worthwhile life. But when we talk about letting God into our lives, there is no such easy unanimity. For many persons, God is a threatening figure. Though seldom put into words, there is a pervasive uneasiness about getting involved with the divine. "If I really give God a place in my life, will that life still be mine? Doesn't the Bible itself talk about a jealous God? To please this jealous God, will I have to surrender the best part of myself? Will I still be free?"

Some religious people may dismiss such fears as unreasonable, even paranoid. But they deserve to be taken seriously. Consider the phenomenon of religion which presumably follows upon one's attempt to relate to God. We must admit that religion does not always enrich its devotees. Some kinds of religiousness make people narrow, insensitive, even bigoted. Less seriously, religion may contribute to unhealthy guilt and a negative self-image and discourage intellectual honesty.

The best way to respond to these objections is to point out that these shortcomings are due not to the nature of God or religion but to people's ignorance and misunderstanding. God wants to enrich me, not impoverish me. Authentic religion does not limit but rather enhances human life. It is meant not to enslave us but to set us free. As Jesus says, "I came so that they might have life and have it more abundantly" (John 10:10). And St. Irenaeus: "The glory of God is a human being fully alive."

Later on we will examine more closely some of these false images of God that strike unreasonable fear in our hearts, try to find out where they came from, and dismiss them once and for all.

There is at least one more obstacle that may get in the way of our efforts to encounter the living God, and which may sound paradoxical at first. It is our tendency to ask for too little from life. If all I want is security, recognition, money, and the things money can buy, why would I need God or religion? The things I want are obtained by hard work, brains, luck, influence, or all four. Then religion can be nothing more than an extra, a peripheral activity that does not touch me at the center of my life, in my values, my commitments, my hopes, and my fears. Until I ask more from life than what the commercials promise, God is superfluous and church is a bore.

All the great religions are attempts to answer humankind's questions of ultimate concern. What is the meaning of life? Is there any transcendent purpose to human existence? Is the human story ultimately comedy or tragedy? What is the strongest force in the universe, life or death? How does a good person behave? These are the questions that thoroughly secularized persons do not ask. They have been pronounced meaningless by materialists of all stripes. They don't even occur to those who have swallowed consumerism as a way of life. Religion, on the other hand, says that God not only answers the deepest questions that we can put to life but also promises the fulfillment of the most profound desires of our hearts. Only when we take such questions seriously and dare to expand our heart wishes can God become not just the answer to a puzzle but the One who alone can satisfy our deepest longings.

Our need for meaning, then, can be truly fulfilled only by union with God and others, and the obstacles to that union are all within ourselves. If we have the will, we can overcome them. How could anyone fail?

Consider the case of the box and the arrow on page 32.

The box is more comfortable than the arrow. By the "box" we mean a nice, comfy, restricted, little place to settle in. It has its own little view of the world that is neat and complete. There is no sense in considering anything outside the box; it would be

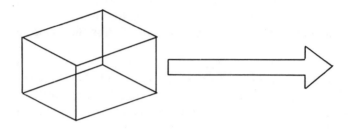

measured only by a ruler found inside the box, so it would not measure up and would be found wanting. The "arrow" isn't comfortable. It involves a probe, a search, a painful birth, a leap, an adventure. Yet it seems to be a law of life that beyond the adventure lies a truer happiness.

Do you really want to get out of your box, with its limited aspirations, and join the arrow to be part of the real, evolving, dynamic world?

As long as you have a restricted vision of your future, you can live in a world where you depend on no one but yourself to attain your limited goals. You are safe, but you may stagnate. If you join the arrow, you leave your zone of safety—the familiar, the manageable, the predictable. But with the risk comes the chance to fulfill your deepest heart wishes.

"All right, but *how* do I get out of the box? And what awaits me when I do? What are the dynamics involved in encountering God and others?" Let's find out.

Things to Do

1. Do Project One and Project Two. Put them in your journal, if you're keeping one. You may keep them to yourself or, if you're part of a group, share some or all of them with the group.
2. As you can see, Project Three is going to be a big part of this whole journey. Do you see this as something to start now, or have you already begun in some way?

4

Opening Up

People need many things, but they need other people most of all. For mere physical survival, things might be enough; but to exist as a human being, you need something more. Some of the wealthiest, most envied people have been the most miserable when they found they could buy everything except human love. Edward Arlington Robinson describes such a person in his poem "Richard Cory":

Whenever Richard Cory went down town,
We people on the pavement looked at him:
He was a gentleman from sole to crown,
Clean favored, and imperially slim.

And he was always quietly arrayed,
And he was always human when he talked;
But still he fluttered pulses when he said,
"Good morning," and he glittered when he walked.

And he was rich—yes, richer than a king—
And admirably schooled in every grace:
In fine, we thought that he was everything
To make us wish that we were in his place.

So on we worked, and waited for the light,
And went without the meat, and cursed the bread;

And Richard Cory, one calm summer night,
Went home and put a bullet through his head.

Richard Cory is a fictional character, but he represents, unfortunately, many more real-life people than we would suspect. He is an extreme example of a malady that afflicts many more in less-spectacular fashion. Why does it happen? Why do so many of us go through life with so much of our capacity for friendship and love unrealized?

It can happen for various reasons. Sometimes we don't know how to make the first move toward others, so failure dogs us from the outset. Sometimes the problem is not forming relationships but coping with the conflicts and other strains that accompany all serious attempts at intimacy. Because of a lack of guidance, some go through life with a minimum of deep human encounters. Early in life they have had a few unhappy experiences and then decided, at some subconscious level, to keep people at a distance for the rest of their lives. They don't want to get hurt again. Or, as we pointed out above, some people simply do not like themselves and avoid offering friendship to others because they feel that they themselves have little or nothing to give. Lacking confidence in themselves, they avoid those situations that might invite rejection.

We are playing for very high stakes here. We need people for more than escaping loneliness and fulfilling our basic need for intimacy. They also help bring out the best in us, to help us realize potentialities in ourselves that might otherwise have lain dormant. It works the other way, too. We can enrich the lives of others, as well. This mutual influence can work wonders. The love a friend has for us, her good example, her desire to make us happy—all help to bring out our good points. Those interesting qualities that make up the real us blossom out, and the same thing is happening to her. We're good for each other. Because of our friendship, each of us is a better person.

God is involved in all this, helping us to influence each other, for God meets us not only directly but also through others. This is one of the central mysteries of life: God encounters people through people.

When we get together, either with God or with others, we

are in a love situation. Earlier, in trying to describe this process of getting together, we used the Japanese word *deai.* It means to go out and then to meet—to encounter. Everyone wants to love and be loved, but love cannot happen unless there is an encounter. There must be a leap out of oneself. And it's scary.

Most of us have many acquaintances but not many friends. It's much easier to become an acquaintance than to become a friend. Becoming an acquaintance is like moving over some flat land. Becoming a friend is like jumping over a deep ditch to someone on the other side.

That leap is scary. One push from the other, and down we go into the ditch. We leap; the other refuses to accept us; down we tumble.

It's not too hard to shake hands with someone. Even though you extend your right hand, you can still protect yourself with your other hand. Most likely, the first two people who shook hands didn't trust each other very much. They were probably holding out their right hands to show they weren't going for their swords.

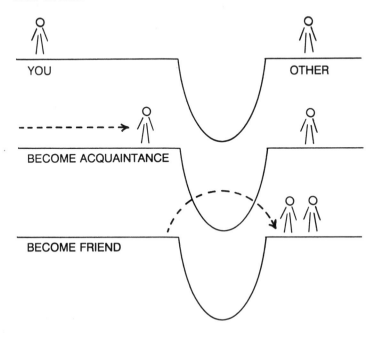

If you go to embrace someone, it's a different story. You're wide open, with no defense. If the other person decides to let you have it, you've had it.

There appears to be a law of life that goes like this:

> Beyond the difficulty
> Beyond the adventure
> Beyond the leap
> Is
> Joy.

There's no denying the difficulty and risk involved in leaping from oneself to the other, but there's no denying the joy that comes with encountering the other.

One reason the leap is difficult is that it involves self-revelation. You have to open up before the other can know you. They can't love what they don't know. You can't fall in love with someone you don't know, nor can anyone love you if they don't know you.

Naturally, revealing yourself isn't easy. It's all part of the leap. It isn't easy to open up the zipper of your heart. "I don't want to share myself. It's the only self I've got."

(By the way, Christians believe that the all-time great self-revelation took place when God was revealed in Jesus Christ by becoming one of us. But more of this later.)

Well, while you're standing there, trying to get up courage to jump, guess what's happening on the other side of the ditch? The other person is probably scared, too, wondering whether to take that leap toward you. Love isn't just a two-way street; it's a two-way jump, too.

Our hearts are like television sets: Take away the antennae, and they don't receive much of anything. We have to keep our antenna out by being interested in others, whether God or other people. We have to think about others, be concerned about them, be open to them. "I wonder if that person is happy or sad. I'd like to get to know that person."

We've known for a long time now that people are not going to come up to us and announce that they would like to love us or be our friends. People are usually more indirect: They send out hints and signals. To pick them up, we have to keep our antenna out.

We have to keep our antenna out to pick up God's signals, too. It's been years since the Lord used the thunder-and-lightning routine. Rather than overwhelm us, God wants us to respond freely to an invitation. The divine voice is usually heard not in thunder and lightning but in the quiet of our heart.

[Elijah] came to a cave, where he took shelter. Then the Lord said, "Go outside and stand on the mountain before the LORD; the LORD will be passing by." A strong and heavy wind was rending the mountains and crushing rocks before the LORD—but the LORD was not in the wind. After the wind there was an earthquake—but the LORD was not in the earthquake. After the earthquake there was fire—but the LORD was not in the fire. After the fire there was a tiny whispering sound. When he heard this, Elijah hid his face in his cloak and went and stood at the entrance of the cave.—1 Kings 19:9, 11-13

"But it's frightening, going out like this and leaving myself wide open. Why not stay in the cave, where it's safe? Suppose I don't leap that ditch? What is there to lose? What is there to gain?"

We know the answer, of course. Loneliness is one of the most painful trials that can befall us. To feel abandoned, isolated, unable to make connections with other men and women is terrifying. This is what we risk when we pursue the illusory goal of total self-sufficiency. There is a part of us that wants to believe we don't need anyone. If we ever let it take over, it can leave us closed in on ourselves, self-absorbed, alone—like Richard Cory.

God, in a mysterious way, is trying to bring you close to others. Many a "chance" meeting results in a deep friendship. A person may be right under your nose for years. You look through each other or settle for a nodding acquaintance. And then one day, mysteriously, you really meet that person. Thanks to God, you encounter other people.

Yet you are no puppet dangling from a string. You are a free, godlike person. You have to go out and seek the other, and you must be willing to receive the other. You must be receptive and ready to venture out, to "leap" toward the other. And when you do, you will know from experience how right that song is:

> People,
> People who need people,
> Are the luckiest people
> In the world.

That's one of the ways we are different from God. God never gets lonely. Why? Because in God's inner life there is an *I* and a *You.* The I is constantly meeting with the You; the You is constantly encountering the I. The I is interested in and loves the You; the You is interested in and loves the I. The I and You share all with each other. This meeting, this love between them, is so intense, so vivid, so strong, so alive, that it's a Person, the Holy Spirit.

We are made like God, but with an important difference. Within me is just the *I.* The *you* is outside. The I within me is always going to seek the you—to want to love and be loved by the you. The you is the other: It's God, it's fellow humans. If I really know myself, then I know that this seeking the you is more basic to me than my own heartbeat.

When I leave the cave and jump the ditch, I leave the illusion of self-sufficiency behind and expose myself to all the risks that go with intimacy. But I also open myself to unlimited possibilities of fulfillment. We get a glimpse of these when we observe some married couples who have matured together. Their love has endured beyond romance and survived the misunderstandings and conflicts, the ups and downs that come to any two people who try to make a life together. He loves her now not just for what she gives him or because she has enriched his life, but just for herself. And she feels the same way about him. Listen to her:

> I like to make him happy, and I try to. When he's happy, so am I. I rejoice in his happiness. When he's sad, I try to help him, to end the sorrow. If there's nothing I can do

(he may be sick, and I'm not a doctor), at least I can share his sorrow.

I like to share not only the extremes of joy or sorrow, but also the ordinary things in his life. Doing something with him, even if it's humdrum, is interesting. I'm interested in his opinions. I may not always agree with them, but I'm interested in them.

And this is the most amazing part of all. He likes to be with me, to make me happy. When I'm happy, he rejoices. When I'm sad, he tries to help. If he can't do anything, at least he'll go half-and-half with my sorrow.

Not only joy and sorrow, but the ordinary things in my life interest him. He wants to share even the humdrum things in my life. When he shares them, they're not so boring anymore. He may not always buy my opinions, but at least he's interested in them. Joy, sorrow, ordinary stuff, you name it, and he's there. Best of all, I know I can count on him. No matter what happens, no matter how bad, he'll stand by me. And he knows I'll stand by him.

This is what real love is all about. What we have here is a dynamic giving-receiving. There's that forgetting of self, that leap toward the other, that giving of self, that self-revelation, that desire to make the other happy. And lo and behold, the other (God or another human being) thinks of me, leaps toward me, reveals and gives of self to me, and wants to make me happy! It bears a remarkable resemblance to the mutual giving and receiving that takes place in the inner life of God.

What is love? We can say three things about it:

- Love is a triangle.
- Love is being able to say, "I know how you feel."
- Love is a campfire.

LOVE IS A TRIANGLE

God is at one corner, you at another, and other people at the third.

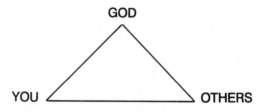

The first thing that happens is that God loves you and loves other people.

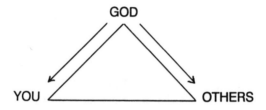

God starts things rolling, makes the first leap. In the beginning we don't love God, who is unknown to us. How can you love someone you don't know? But God doesn't get discouraged, any more than the parents of a newborn child get discouraged. The parent loves the child right from the start, but it's a one-way street. All the baby wants is to be fed, burped, and changed. The child doesn't love the parent, but the parent is in no hurry, for gradually the child will get to know the parent, and in knowing, begin to love in return. What starts out as a one-way street gradually becomes a two-way love relationship.

It's the same with God, who doesn't get discouraged and keeps on loving. In time, you and others will get to know and thus come to love God. What started out as a one-way street will gradually become a mutual love relationship.

It's God who brings us together in this life. Thanks to God, you have many wonderful meetings with other people in your life. It's because of the love you receive from God that you have the ability to love others. It's because of the love others receive from God that they have the ability to love you.

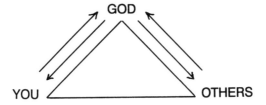

In the beginning you may not love God, you may not know or even advert to God, and yet you go around loving other people. Though you may not be aware of it, God is loving you every day, and that is why you're able to love others. Just as we turn on a light switch and never advert to the generator that's producing the electricity, it's because of the generator that the light goes on. Of course, what we're dealing with here is not some generator in the sky but a loving, personal God. And so, thanks to God, we love one another.

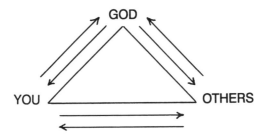

Just one more point. You can't love without being loved. If you cut yourself off from receiving love, you may still be able to love for a short time, but you're going to dry up very soon.

LOVE IS BEING ABLE TO SAY, "I KNOW HOW YOU FEEL"

Imagine that you're going to Japan, not as a tourist, but to live there with the people for five years.

When you go to Japan this way, you die and have to be born

again. You leave America as a relatively educated person and enter Japan as a dummy, an idiot, a barbarian.

You don't know how to eat (chopsticks). Even if you do, you're not too sure you want to (today's special: raw fish). You don't know how to sit (on your ankles on the floor; it hurts). You don't know how to go into a house (take your shoes off, dummy). You don't know how to take a bath (wash before you get into the boiling water, you idiot). If you want to go shopping, someone has to take you, because with your lack of Japanese, you could easily get lost. You're a barbarian specializing in social blunders from morning to night.

Because the Japanese language is so complicated, you find yourself in a strange situation. It's as though you were standing in a doorway with a series of closed doors on your left and right. The doors are labeled: expression of past experiences, expression of present emotions, expression about history, expression about literature, expression about life, expression about love. On each door are two locks. One has been opened by training and experience in America. The other can be opened only by knowing the Japanese language. As yet, you can't open it, so you stand humiliated, alone, and lonely in the hallway.

Gradually, of course, you begin to learn the language (which you continue to learn for the rest of your life). It is, however, complicated. Ordinarily, the subject of the sentence is not expressed (Who did what?), singular or plural is not expressed (the same word is used for one friend or ten friends). Gender is not expressed; someone can talk to you about a third person for ten minutes and you still may not know if it's a man or woman. And so it goes.

So what happens? After a lot of sweat you can talk about many things. You can go shopping, talk about the weather, take a trip without getting lost, order in a restaurant. That's progress, all right, but a big problem remains. Although you are functioning in the language, it is still so complicated that it may take you up to four years before you can have a heart-to-heart talk with anyone. Now this is a heavy cross, because you are a people person. There's so much you want to say! There's so much you want to hear! It's as though you were in an isolation booth, surrounded by people, and dying of loneliness.

When you go to Japan, you die and have to be born again.

And then when another newcomer arrives and says, "I'm confused," you can say, "I know how you feel." He may confide in you and tell you, "This whole bit is new, confusing, scary." And you know what he is talking about—not just in your head, but in your guts. She tells you, "I'm lonely." You say, "I know what you're talking about." You can share her feelings the way no one else can who has not actually experienced them.

You don't have to go to Japan to share an emotion with someone. You can do it anywhere, with anyone, in any situation. Here's how:

• *Recall your own experience.* It doesn't have to be identical with the other's experience, just similar—a sorrow, a hurt, a confusion, a loneliness.

• *Feel with the other.* This is what the word *sympathy* meant originally—not to "feel sorry for," but to "feel with" the other. I may feel sorry for that poor guy who got hit by the car, but if I've never been in an accident, I cannot feel the way he does.

• *Share the experience or feeling* with the other. The other, in some way, can give you a part of it. He or she is no longer alone.

Here are some other points to keep in mind:

• The experience or emotion doesn't have to be a difficult one. It can be a joy, a happiness, a surprise, a hope.

• You can be the one with the experience or emotion, and someone can share it with you.

• When God entered the human condition, it became possible to share our experiences and emotions. God knows how we feel.

LOVE IS LIKE A CAMPFIRE

Love is not like a pie; it's like a campfire. Some people think love is like a pie, with just so many slices. There's a slice for God, a slice for husband or wife, a few slices for the kids, and a few slices for others.

"Sorry, God, but if I give you a bigger slice, there just won't be enough to go around. Sorry, wife or husband, but you know how it is. If I give you a bigger slice, everyone else goes short. What are you yelling about, kids? You're getting your slices, aren't you? Sorry, all you people out there, but aside from a few of you, there are no more slices to go around!"

The source of love — any love — is God. God is infinite, without any limits, while we're limited. But our capacity to love and be loved can grow, which is why it's like a campfire.

To start a campfire, you begin small, with a few twigs. Once you get these lit, you put on some wood that's a little bigger. And once that catches fire and is burning nicely, you add bigger and bigger wood, until you're using logs. Now we have a real campfire going, and if we feel like it, we can build it up into a bonfire.

Inside you there's a fire waiting to be lit. The more you love, the greater is your capacity to love. The more you love God, the more you're able to love people around you. And the more you love them, the more you're able to love God. The more you love your wife or husband, the more you're able to love the kids. The more you love your kids, the more you're able to love your husband or wife. The more you love family, the more you can love others. The more you love others, the more you can love family.

That's the difference between pies and campfires. The more wood you throw on a campfire, the more wood it can absorb. And it's nice to know that the more you're loved, the more you're capable of being loved.

One more thing about campfires: If you don't throw more wood on them, they gradually subside and go out. Maybe that's what happened to Richard Cory. Most likely his life didn't lack for intimacy at first. In his youth there were probably friendships, maybe even love, but he failed to grow, to meet the challenge that comes to all of us in our mature years. Erik Erikson calls it the crisis of generativity when we are called to nurture others, to care in some way for the next generation. The alternative is stagnation as described by Francis Gross in his book *Introducing Erik Erikson* (pp. 55-56):

> The word "stagnant" carries with it an image of decay, of rotting. A stagnant pond has a bad smell. So does a stagnant person. In a withering description of stagnation in a

person of mature years, Erikson says that a person whose life is stagnant seems to treat himself as though he himself were his own children. There is a quality of self-centeredness, sometimes demanding total order in a home, obsessed with the small details of living. Frequently, there is a gnawing overconcern with one's health. Think of a woman whose makeup is never smeared, whose house is never messy, who is dominated by the latest health fad, the new doctor in town, the exact right amount of vitamins per meal. Think of a man who can't stand being called at the office, who erupts if he doesn't see every play of a televised football game, who is either always impeccably dressed or always embarrassingly shabby and slovenly, whose routine is either totally rigid, or who has no routine at all.

In any case, regardless of detail, we are talking about a middle-aged person whose sun rises and sets on himself. If the reader is of this age and feels a bit queasy at finding something of his own life here, then it is again time to remind that reader that there is no Generativity without the experience of Stagnation. No one who is a caring person has emerged with that vital strength without periods of Stagnation. The battle between these two enemies is never over; nor could one exist without the other.

In one of his later works, Erikson mentions that he realized in his own middle years how frequently the quality of Stagnation is marked by a terrible and punitive anger.

Maybe Richard Cory lost that battle and finally directed his terrible anger at himself.

One last word. Before any of these fires get lit, before we take any leaps toward others, there's one indispensable condition: You cannot love other persons or God unless you love one person in particular. Can you guess who?

Who else but yourself?

God says you must love your neighbor as yourself. When we hear that, we usually start thinking about our neighbors—who they are and whether we can love them. We take that second part, "as yourself," for granted. And why not? Don't all people love themselves too much?

Sometimes, but not very often. You might be surprised to know how many people don't like what they see in the mirror. We're not talking about faults and failings. It's natural to dislike our failings. We're talking about people who don't like *themselves*. They're really unhappy being in their own presence; they really don't love themselves.

If you don't like your face or your figure or your faults, that's all right. But if you don't love your*self,* then you can't love God or others, either. Why? Well, when you love somebody, what you're doing is giving yourself as a gift to that person. If you don't love yourself, then you rate yourself as nothing, and you have nothing to give.

When you think of it, isn't that Charlie Brown's problem? The underlying reason why he doesn't cross the schoolyard and say hello to the little redheaded girl is that he thinks he's a nothing. He can't relate because he thinks he has nothing to give.

If you do love yourself, then what you're saying when you love someone is: "Here, I give you myself. I'm not perfect. I'm not the greatest thing since canned beer. But I'm all I've got, and I give it to you."

Things to Do

1. A genuine human encounter involves a leap that is sometimes scary. Have you ever made such a leap? Did you end up in the ditch or on the other side?
2. Were you ever surprised to find a different side, or a new depth, in a person you thought you knew?
3. Love is being able to say, "I know how you feel." Have you ever learned this from experience?
4. Pick out one sad story in your life, one human encounter that turned out badly. What happened? What went wrong? How did it affect you? Does the memory linger on?
5. Have you ever felt within yourself the battle between generativity and stagnation?
6. Why is it that some people don't like themselves?

5

False Gods

By this time, you know a lot about encountering others. That's one half of religious experience. The other half, encountering God, isn't so very different. The same rules that make for healthy human relationships—keeping the antennae out, being willing to take scary leaps, building campfires of love—apply to the way we meet and come to know and love God. And yet there are obstacles that may keep us from encountering and achieving union with God. By the same token, if we can recognize these obstacles and overcome them, we may go a long way toward finding not only ourselves and other people but also the God who loves us, gives us life, and brings us together.

What are these obstacles? They are many, but they come under four basic headings: doubt, unconcern, disappointment, and fear.

DOUBT AND UNCONCERN

Most reflective people, even those from religious backgrounds, sometimes doubt the existence of God. Atheists have resolved the matter for themselves. They work from the principle of "What you see is what you get." Since they cannot see God, they readily conclude that God does not exist. They offer various explanations for the pervasive phenomenon of religion, but these all come down to some form of illusion. Agnostics are less dogmatic. They admit that there may be a God, but believe that we can never really know for sure. The practical conclusion

47

is a kind of functional atheism, living as if God did not exist.

The hesitations of agnostics are not foreign to religious people, either. Some of the greatest saints have gone through periods of interior darkness when God seemed absent, even unreal. Because the full reality of God is not totally demonstrable by purely rational arguments or by the methods proper to physical science, believers will always be vulnerable to this kind of doubt. It doesn't happen to everyone, but no one should be surprised if it does happen.

A much greater obstacle than doubt, at least in our time and culture, is unconcern. Perhaps a better word to describe it is inattentiveness. The source is secularization, a tendency to perceive and relate to our world of experience without any reference to its spiritual dimension. Secularization has been variously defined, but Harvey Cox's description is probably the best. For him the secularized person is one for whom life is not a mystery but a series of problems and projects. The thoroughly secularized person's attention and energies are completely taken up with the practical affairs and demands of life. Questions of larger meaning or transcendent purpose, such as the ones asked by Caroline in chapter one, are not only not addressed, they are not even adverted to. Thus God, the One who for believers answers their questions of ultimate concern, does not even appear on the stage of consciousness, which is too cluttered with other players to leave any room.

Is there such a thing as a completely secularized person? It is an interesting question that is debated from time to time. More importantly, it is obvious that many people are secularized to a greater or lesser degree. We all know people like this. They are often decent, caring people who are trying to lead responsible lives in ways that, at least in conventional terms, are not religious. Even more to the point is the impact that secularization has on us. Rare is the person, in a culture like ours, who is not touched by it. Our lives are filled with so many things that we sometimes get the feeling that God is crowded out, not only of our priorities, but even of our awareness.

The impact of secularization on people's capacity for religious experience is greatly increased by the phenomenon of consumerism. Advertising, the propaganda instrument of consumer culture, assures us, implicitly but insistently, that products can satisfy our deepest human needs. Even the language of transcendence ("You're in good hands") is co-opted by commercials that guarantee not only beauty and pleasure but also vitality, success, intimacy, love, and security. They promise to dispel our darkest fears and fulfill our fondest hopes. Are any of us completely immune to these messages? To the extent that we are touched by them, it becomes harder for us to reach out toward God. St. Augustine said that our hearts are restless until they rest in God. If he were alive today, he would be astounded at the ability of the forces of mass culture to still that restlessness or divert it.

DISAPPOINTMENT

Sometimes the problem is not a reluctance to try religion, but a feeling that it has been tried and hasn't worked. Many have dabbled in various kinds of religion and quasi-religious self-help programs; some have even been deeply involved. But after a while the enthusiasm waned, disillusionment set in, and they turned their attention elsewhere. When these excursions into religiosity lead nowhere, they may leave one with an understandable reluctance to try any new brand of spiritual snake oil. George Sim Johnson, a baby boomer, paints a vivid picture of the religious scene on campus in his undergraduate days in the early seventies ("Everything Goes, Nothing Matters," pp. 19-20):

The point of the mantra, apart from putting me in touch with the infinite Ground of Being, was to make me feel well-adjusted, healthy, at ease with things. This was a major undergraduate preoccupation at the time. All were busy getting their heads together ... Dropping out for a semester, they would pack a copy of *The Prophet* and a few James Taylor albums and head for Cape Cod or some other vale of Kashmir. Generally they came back more crazed than ever. But the quest never abated. The goal was an interior peace that could be manipulated like the graphic equalizer on a sound system. This, I submit, is the great and seldom-achieved prize of modern secular culture, and it is not surprising that the search for it is often conducted through a maze of religiosity.

Disappointment with religion sometimes has quite different, more respectable roots. A religious childhood in a mainline church, where for one reason or another the connections were never made, can leave one with a chip on the shoulder. If our childhood memories of church and prayer summon up only negative feelings, it is hard to listen with an open mind and heart. It's a bit as if we were forced to read Shakespeare as ten-year-olds and swore off the stuff for life.

FEAR

Although doubt, unconcern, and disappointment present formidable obstacles to encountering God, they probably do not have as great an influence as fear. We are not talking here about the fear of being punished for our misdeeds but about something much more basic. As we have written elsewhere (*So You Want to Do Ministry*, p. 54):

God, for many people, is not just mysterious or elusive or problematic . . . but downright *threatening*. Besides being a riddle or puzzle that is hard for the mind to encompass or accept, God assaults the emotions with feelings of disquiet and even fear. This is not exactly the same phenomenon as Rudolph Otto's *mysterium tremendum et fascinans*. It is something much more negative, often beneath the level of consciousness, which can stifle the religious impulse in its cradle. It is the oft-unspoken fear that if we find God we will lose the best part of ourselves. Unlike thoroughly secularized persons who see religion as superfluous, these see it as a potential impoverishment of the self. To them, religion is not just a mistaken world view but a negative force that can make us less human.

But how can an encounter with God be considered an impoverishment? It can if it is perceived as depriving the subject of something important. What are the things that we are afraid of losing if we get too close to God?

First of all, we may be afraid that if God comes into our lives some other things that don't belong there may have to go. None of us likes to confront ourselves this way. We don't want to give up our selfishness, our laziness, our creature comforts that don't belong, or a practice or relationship that doesn't belong—that contradicts what we stand for. Of course, we know in our heart of hearts that these things make us poorer and that we would be enriched if God helped us get rid of them. But we love our chains and resist having to give them up. Conversely, there may be something missing in our lives that belongs there. If God is allowed into our lives, unwelcome reminders of these sins of omission are sure to follow. Thus our sinfulness makes cowards of us and obliges us to keep God at arm's length. If this is what holds us back, then we must pray for courage and trust: courage to open ourselves to something better, and trust that God will more than make it up to us.

A second deprivation that is sometimes feared is the sacrifice of intelligence. During one memorable episode of the television series "All in the Family," Archie Bunker makes an assertion based on his fuzzy understanding of religion. His atheist son-in-law, Michael, derides his statement as unfounded and asks what evidence he has. Archie fires back: "It's faith, Meathead! Can't you understand that? Faith is what makes you believe what no person in his right mind would say."

In his own muddled way, Archie is giving voice to the anti-intellectual strain that has always been a prominent feature of much of American religion. Some think of religion as competing with logic and intellectual honesty and wonder: "Can I take God seriously and still be a cultivated person of the twentieth and twenty-first centuries?"

Archie, for all his ignorance, is on to something: Life is bigger than the human mind can comprehend; ultimately it's a mystery that borders on the infinite. As Hamlet reminds Horatio, "There are more things in heaven and earth than are dreamt of in your philosophy." Unfortunately, some surrender too much: They confuse going *beyond* reason with going *against* reason. Those who fear that God may demand the sacrifice of rationality must be reassured that God, who gave us our reason, will never ask us to betray it. Contrary to popular prejudice, being smart is not an obstacle to union with God.

Another fear that can keep us from reaching out to God is that of becoming less human. It is an incontrovertible fact that religion makes some people rigid, dogmatic, authoritarian, or intolerant. Mary McCarthy, a lapsed Catholic, once observed that Roman Catholicism was a dangerous faith for any but the most balanced personalities; for the others, it was likely to exaggerate their worst features. This should not scandalize us. Jesus himself encountered the most intense opposition from men of deep but distorted religious conviction. The only honest response to this fear is to remember that while religion can and sometimes does make its adherents spooky, it doesn't have to.

IT'S ALL RIGHT TO GROW UP

An even more common challenge to the religious impulse is the unspoken fear that God may be the enemy of maturity. It was Sigmund Freud who called religion not only an illusion but, more seriously, an infantile regression. Though the charge is false, it does have some prima facie evidence to support it. Religious faith is commonly and correctly associated, in people's minds, with such qualities as obedience, docility, and submission. Not so commonly associated with faith are such characteristics as independence, initiative, creativity, and autonomy. Yet the latter qualities are proper to adulthood, while the former are normally linked to childhood dependence. Consider the creation myth, the so-called Adam and Eve story in the Book of Genesis, which has powerfully influenced our religious imagery. Ask any group of people with even a rudimentary church background what God's first command was to the man and the woman, and most will reply, "Do not eat of the forbidden fruit." As a matter of fact, a closer examination of the text reveals that God's first directive is to till the garden, name the animals, and take charge of their world. The original transgression is not disobedience but a failure to take responsibility. Cox describes it as the sin of letting a snake tell them what to do.

All kinds of hangovers flow from this misapprehension of God and faith and what faith entails. Consider the two young women in their twenties who explained to an inquiring reporter why they don't go to church anymore. One said that she didn't believe in religion, she believed in herself. The other explained that she didn't have to lean on religion, she could think for herself. These two women clearly see God as a threat to their adulthood. But who said that we must make a choice between believing in God or believing in ourselves? Where is it written that God does not want us to think for ourselves? The God revealed in Jesus Christ is One who wants us to use our intelligence, cultivate our gifts, and fulfill our possibilities. This God wants us to take responsibility not only for ourselves but for our world, to organize it in just and peaceful fashion and to care for one another.

So where does this fear come from? From one of two sources, one within the person and one outside. Within some people is a longing for unlimited autonomy. They want to be accountable to no one. Their idea of freedom is being under no constraint whatever. The very notion of any law or authority that might put limits on them is intolerable. They will submit to society's laws for reasons of self-interest, but any moral considerations beyond legality strike them as the arbitrary impositions of a coercive authoritarianism.

From outside the person there may be a very different source—those who believe in and try to serve God in socially irresponsible ways. Their God is the God of the status quo, the guarantor of law and order and of peace at any price, including systemic injustice. This God is enthroned in the churches of Third World societies where the obscenely wealthy can worship without being reminded of the destitute hordes at their gates. A century ago Karl Marx railed at the churches who preached this kind of God who guaranteed the ill-gotten gains of the privileged and consoled the masses with promises of pie in the sky by and by when they died. Marxism is now out of fashion, but the Marxist critique of religion is still very much alive.

When we become sensitive to the demands of justice in a world where unjust political, social, and economic structures are propped up and legitimated by a world-denying ideology masquerading as religion, the God of the pseudofaith can become intolerable. Three thousand years ago the prophets of Israel inveighed against these rationalizations of selfishness, and modern-day prophets still speak out against them and still get the same mixed reviews.

In reaching out to God, you must be clear in your mind that God is interested not only in your soul but in *you*. God wants to relate to you as a whole, as a person, and not just to some so-called segment of you. God doesn't have a split vision of you with an important part (soul) and a less-important part (body). Nor does God have a split vision of your life (a religious part, a nonreligious part). God wants to relate to the whole you and to the whole of your life. This is not only the God of the prayer, the church, the Eucharist. This is also the God of the dance, the job, the home, the plans.

Of course, it works the other way, too. If you get involved with this God, you will be asked to care about people in the same way. Religion will come to mean not only trying to get to heaven but also trying to make a better world here and now for everyone, especially for those who are left out. That's a bit scary, too. Who among us wants to take on more responsibility? But God not only enlarges our horizons but our hearts, as well, to make room for all God's children.

There is at least one more fear that may deter us from trying to encounter God: the fear that we may lose our individuality. Like most of the fears already described, this one is rarely put into words. It is the nameless fear of meeting a higher level of existence. This may explain why many people feel threatened by God. They acknowledge that God is good, but they want to keep their distance. There's the unspoken fear that if God gets too close (or if they should get "spiritual" and too close to God), their humanity, their personality, their individuality will suffer. Remember those science-fiction movies where they invent this blob in the laboratory and it breaks free? The next thing you know, it's rolling down the street and absorbing everything in its path. Maybe God is like a spiritual blob that will just roll over us and swallow up our individuality and leave just a great big zero. This may well be the feeling of many people, although they've never actually put it into words. But God does not act that way. The person becomes more of a person, the individual more of an individual. Far from being swallowed up by contact with God, one's humanity, personality, and individuality are increased.

FALSE SOLUTIONS, FALSE GODS

These are some of the fears that keep us from encountering God. They are all ultimately groundless because they tell us nothing about God, only about ourselves. They also show the wisdom of the saying that fear is the little darkroom where negatives are developed. Once we expose these chimeras for what they are, the way is open for a love affair between God and us. But they must be confronted and disposed of, or else we may react not by rejecting religion altogether but by setting up in God's place a false deity that we can live with. We will then have the trappings of authentic religion without the reality. Two familiar versions of this false God immediately come to mind.

The first is the God of Deism, also known as the Watchmaker God. In this secularized version of Christianity, God is the ultimate answer to the puzzle of existence. The deist looks at the world around her, reasons about the ultimate meaning of it all, then concludes that there must be a First Cause who made all this. But, as far as she can see, that is all. God made the world, wound it up like a watch, set it going, and then left it alone. This God is not involved in reality, does not intervene in any way, indeed is not interested enough to intrude on creation. This faceless deity, sometimes referred to by theologians as the God of the Philosophers, is the product of reason and appeals to nothing more than reason. It makes no claim on our emotions or our allegiance. Its only function is to provide an intellectually satisfying solution to the question of the origin of the universe.

Historians of the United States will recognize this God as the one referred to by our nation's founding fathers in the Declaration of Independence. Those men wrote eloquently of a Creator who had endowed us with inalienable rights—a Creator whom Christians acknowledged as the God revealed in Jesus. But those men were not involved in Christianity, properly so-called. They did not believe in divine revelation or the influence of God's grace. Theirs was a secularized version of faith, spawned by the rationalism of the Enlightenment and living off the spiritual capital left by centuries of Christian tradition.

There is a good deal of evidence that Deism is very much alive today. James Heft, a professor of theology, says that many young people from a religious background are deists without realizing it. For them, Christianity is a philosophy from Jesus which helps them develop a way of life. But their unstated presupposition is that God will not intervene. As far as they can see, God doesn't *do* anything; it's all up to them. When these undergraduates work out their goals and projects, they first set out the agenda and then ask God's help. They don't let God in on the setting of the agenda. It doesn't take much imagination to see that such a do-nothing God is not restricted to college campuses. By now it should be clear that it is a far cry from the God that Jesus and we are talking about.

The second false God doesn't have a name like the God of the deists, perhaps because of a rather recent arrival on the scene. This is the God who doesn't make junk, who likes us just the way we are and wouldn't want us to change a thing. The main function of this God is to affirm us and shore up our self-image. If we feel guilty or otherwise bad about ourselves, this God assures us that we're really okay. The well-meaning people who preach and teach this version of God are fond of telling us that we are unconditionally loved. This is true, of course. Jesus assures us that no matter what we do, our Father will never stop loving us. Unfortunately, some people draw the conclusion that God loves us so much as not to care what we do.

One of the authors met this easygoing God in a teenage girl's statement explaining why she rejected the church's teaching against premarital sex. She wrote: "God gave us life and told us that he would not stand in the way, and would let us make our own decisions. Individuals should be the ones to dictate to themselves what their opinion on premarital sex is."

This second false God resembles in some ways the God described by Jesus. Love, care, encouragement, affirmation, and respect for freedom come through very clearly. What is missing? Challenge, judgment, and idealism. There is no call to conversion here, just a bland assurance that we should feel good about ourselves. This God is never allowed to surprise us. It is a long way from the God who says, through Isaiah, "My ways are not your ways." This is a domesticated God who would never want to disturb us, unlike the God of Jesus, who not only comforts the afflicted but also occasionally afflicts the comfortable.

Once we have dispelled false fears about God and have resisted the temptation to enthrone an ersatz God, made to our own specifications, we are ready to encounter the true God. Or, rather, we are ready to respond to God, who—while we have been clearing away the underbrush—has all this time been reaching out and waiting for us.

Things to Do

1. Did you recognize any of the false Gods described here?
2. Are there other false Gods that we left out?
3. What do you consider the greatest obstacle to faith: doubt, unconcern, disappointment, or fear?
4. Have you ever felt any of the fears described here?

6

The Real God

We spent most of the last chapter clearing away the underbrush, removing the artificial obstacles and misunderstandings that keep us from encountering God. Now that the false and imaginary Gods have been disposed of, will the real God please stand up? No, that's the wrong question. God has been standing up all the while. The question is, are we ready to stand up? Are we willing to encounter the real God?

If you are, then in a real sense this book is working for you. In fact, you may be even further along than that. Maybe God has been real and present to you for as long as you can remember. Or perhaps in the course of reading and using this book, doing the exercises, seeking and sharing and taking chances, you may have already experienced to some extent what we have been talking about. By this time, God may have become for you more than a word, more than a rumor started by someone else; indeed, a part of your own personal, private world.

Or maybe you can remember a time, long ago, when God was very real to you. But that was before your faith ran out and God disappeared from your personal horizon. Maybe you fell victim to the classic difficulty of the cultural Christian. The cultural Christian is someone who is born into a Christian family, brought up in the church, and taught the Christian religion without ever going through a process of personal conversion.

In order to understand why this can be a problem, consider for a moment how a child learns her native language. First she speaks the language; much later, she learns the grammar.

Because she follows a natural order of learning, she is able to communicate well (though perhaps not in a grammatically correct fashion) in her native language with others. The case of adults who take up a second language is quite different. Depending on the method of instruction, they may find themselves concentrating on the grammar rules rather than on the actual speaking of the language. As a result, while they may be grammatically correct, they don't communicate well with others in this language. You can probably verify this from your own experience, especially if you've studied a foreign language in high school. French or German grammar can tie you up in knots, and speaking those languages may come very hard. How much easier it was to learn English! You were talking a blue streak before anybody even told you about grammar, because you learned the natural way.

Well, there appears to be a "natural" order in the faith encounter with God, too. When it's reversed, as sometimes happens with the cultural Christian, the person may be technically correct about the many "somethings" involved—the doctrines, the laws, the Bible stories—but may not communicate well with the Someone involved. Such a person knows the prayers, the right words, the gestures, but has no *feel* for it. He or she has mastered the "grammar" of religion but can't communicate, and without communication, without encounter, religion is just words, words, words.

Put it another way: We normally believe *someone* before we believe *something.* We are reluctant to believe what strangers tell us, especially in matters of importance. If that stranger becomes an acquaintance, we may find it a little easier to take his or her word for something. But if a deep friendship gradually develops between you, your willingness to believe this person is greatly increased. The closer you get to someone, the more you are able to believe the something he or she tells you.

Now look at the experience of a person who is not born a Christian but is converted to the faith as a teenager or adult. At first God is a stranger. Who can believe a stranger? Then someone or some event introduces them to God, who becomes an acquaintance. Gradually an intimate friendship develops with a personal God. Now the person believes Someone and is prepared to believe something on that someone's word. It's only when a newcomer has an experience of a personal God that things start to happen. One encounters God, believes in God, then believes what God says.

For many of us, the experience is quite different. We are baptized as infants. As we grow up, there seems to be an over-emphasis on the many somethings we are supposed to believe, and the Someone gets lost. We know a lot of religion, but we've never really met God. But once we have cleared up the mis-understandings and overcome the fears brought on by false images of God, we may be ready for a real encounter with the real God. At this point it is good to remember that faith between you and God is very much like a marriage. If he wants to get married but she doesn't, no marriage. If she's ready but he isn't, those wedding bells won't chime. Faith is the same; it takes two.

God takes a shine to you, approaches, and opens up to you. But if you're not buying, nothing happens. God finds you very interesting, likes you a lot, and will probably try again, but leaves it up to you. God doesn't want you unless you're free. On the other hand, you cannot arrive at a faith encounter all by yourself. It takes two for a friendship, for a marriage, for a faith encounter. It's nice to know that even when we are not ready, God is always ready and willing to encounter us. That doesn't mean that we should take God for granted, just that God is more patient with us than we are with ourselves.

How would you describe your own situation? Maybe it hasn't happened yet, but you are open to the experience of meeting the living God. Or perhaps you have an already developed relationship with God. In either case, it is worth exploring the dynamics involved in this most mysterious and profound of all relationships. The more you understand about God and yourself and the inner workings of religious experience, the better chance you have of achieving close union with God and thus fulfilling to the limit your possibilities as a person.

How does it feel to encounter God? Everyone is different, and no two people encounter or relate to God in exactly the same way. The possibilities and variations are limitless. Some experience God as simply *being with* them. There is a deep-down awareness of the Lord as Presence, supporting, caring, consoling. For others, the encounter means feeling *called.* God has summoned me, and I have responded. There's the feeling that God made the first move, that before I chose God, God chose me. Why, I can't explain.

This doesn't mean that God loves me instead of others, or at their expense. No, God loves them, too. And yet there is something special about this presence, about this call. God has made a personal, individual, free choice of me. No matter how many people are involved, God doesn't choose people in bunches, but one by one, and by name.

On the other hand, just because God chose me doesn't mean that I'm the greatest thing around. Why me? Because I'm the best or the most? No. Well, then why? So don't ask. Look, love is mysterious. The heart has its own reasons. Why do you love the people you do—because they're the richest, the smartest, the handsomest, the most talented? No, love doesn't work that way, thank God! So don't ask why God loves you. Respect the mystery and accept the fact in gratitude and awe.

There's another side to this experience. Not only is the person chosen by God; in a real sense, she or he chooses God, too. It takes two to make an encounter, to form a friendship, to seal a marriage. An encounter is based on love, and love is based on freedom. As God freely chooses us, so we freely choose God. This doesn't mean we're not afraid. Ever watch the bridegroom at a wedding? He's trying to look cool, but no one is fooled.

Once the person answers the call and chooses freely to respond, you might think that all is well. The wedding is over, and all that remains is to live together happily ever after. But in real life, marriages don't work that way. Neither do friendships, and neither do relationships between ourselves and God.

Many people in their encounter with God find themselves in a bind. On the one hand, they may be hurting, yet God seems to be indifferent, hiding from them, ignoring their pain, so they feel angry. On the other hand, they have been told that God is perfect, wears a white hat, and is all-good, all-just, all-merciful. How can you get mad at a perfect God? So they're stuck with their anger and their pain, and are not even supposed to feel it.

Some people see this problem as insoluble and withdraw from all God relations. They have a spokesman in a famous passage from *The Brothers Karamazov*. Ivan, a special kind of atheist, is outraged at the bad things that happen to good people, so he tells Alyosha, his religious brother: "It's not God that I deny. I just reject his world, and most respectfully return him the ticket." Others may not think the matter out so clearly. All they know is that over a period of time their relations with God have gone downhill.

It is important to remember that our perceptions of God are limited. God is infinite and perfect, but I may not experience God that way. In my limited fashion, the God that I know is a God who seems to hide, who seems to let me down sometimes, who seems to be uninterested in me. If I feel let down, I should let God know how I feel about it. It doesn't matter if my words are not the finest. If a person I hardly know lets me down, well, I chalk it up to experience. But if I feel that someone I count on, someone I'm trying to love, someone I think loves me, ignores me and lets me down, I'm going to tell that person about it, and the words may not be nice.

Getting angry at God may be hard to do. It may violate an unspoken taboo deep within me. But what happens is that the boil is lanced; the anger, hurt, loneliness, frustration come forth, and there can be healing. A much more important thing may also be happening. Perhaps for the first time in my life, I'm relating to God as a Person and not as an abstraction.

The wife of a young policeman died, together with her son, in childbirth. A young priest, trying to be compassionate, told him, "If God was going to pick a flower, he would pick the sweetest of them all." The husband replied, "Tell God to go to hell." Three years later, in a nursing home, he saw a young woman who had suffered massive brain damage from a stroke. Her husband brought her flowers, but she did not even know what they were. At that moment the policeman realized that if his wife had lived, she would have been like that. Fourteen years and several jobs later, he was ordained a priest at the age of forty-two.

Anger at God is not some new, shocking idea. The Psalms, written under God's inspiration, have many expressions of it. Their original language, Hebrew, dealt mostly in terms of black and white and didn't bother much with shades of gray, so when the psalmist in the original Hebrew was mad at God, he was really mad! English, on the other hand, has many fine distinctions and shades of gray, so when the Psalms are translated into English, they are toned down somewhat.

When you feel free enough to talk frankly to God, you are ready for a relationship that is not only vertical but also horizontal. No matter how high an opinion you may have of yourself, you know that God is greater than you. Hence you relate "up" to God. Yet if this is a love encounter, there's another relationship, which we may term face-to-face. Lovers, no matter what their difference in rank (and this includes the Creator and the creature), also meet as equals. There's an equality to love that brings the two eye-to-eye, face-to-face.

Encounterers, of course, relate "up" to God. At the same time, though, they are relaxed and enjoy God's company. They speak freely and don't worry about fancy words. They're not afraid to let God know, in plain language, when they feel let down. They relate to a God whom they love and who loves them, face-to-face. (Wouldn't this face-to-face relationship be tremendously enhanced if God were ever to become a human being?)

One-on-one; I and thou. Do we really know God this way? Isn't God's face obscure, hidden in shadows? "At present we see indistinctly, as in a mirror, but then face-to-face. At present I know partially; then I shall know fully, as I am fully known" (1 Corinthians 13:12).

Encounterers want God to be revealed. They don't expect visions, but they realize that they can't love what they don't know. They know you can't begin to love someone unless you meet and experience that someone. And so they pray, "God, please reveal yourself to me. What are you like? Will the real God please stand up? What are your thoughts, your feelings, your experiences? What do you think of yourself? What are you really like? The philosophers tell me that you are the source of truth and goodness and beauty and love and life. That statement means nothing to me. I want to *experience* your goodness, your beauty, your truth, your love, your life. Lord, please reveal yourself to me, and continue to do so."

You want to know God not just with your mind, but with your

whole self. This is the knowledge of union. But union with God involves a twofold mystery.

The first part of this mystery is that in this union you are continually entering deeper and deeper into the life of God. This is more than a pious statement. In this union you and God are truly one. Did you ever notice how you want to hug someone you love? You want to become one with that person. Even a very young child holds out its arms to embrace and be embraced. She may not even be able to talk yet, but she knows that desire to be one with the beloved. The embrace, the being one, the union between you and God, is not just a hug of a few seconds. It is deeper and closer than you can possibly imagine, and it can grow deeper and closer every day.

The second part of this mystery is that you are you. You and God are one, and yet (mystery!) you are you. You are eternal. You will always be you. You are unique. There never was, there isn't now, nor will there ever be, another you. There's something special and interesting about you, simply because you are you. You are never going to be smothered, never going to be absorbed. The intimate oneness between yourself and God is compatible with the fact that you are a unique person and always will be.

What lies ahead for you and God as your friendship grows and deepens? And what can you do to nourish that relationship? How can you stay close?

Here are a few suggestions. Most of them apply to any human relationship and would help any friendship along. A few apply in a special way to our friendship with God.

Try Not to Take God for Granted

Beware of the "sponge" gratitude that is really ingratitude. It's easy to absorb all the good things God gives us and go our merry, thoughtless way. Jesus cured ten lepers and only one came back to thank him. That's inexcusable.

If, like the one grateful leper, you remember to say thank you, don't do it in the spirit of "balancing the books." You know what we mean. Some of us don't like the idea of anyone, even God, being one up on us. Jesus tells this story about a Pharisee praying in the Temple: "O God, I thank you that I am not like the rest of humanity . . . I fast . . . I give to charity . . . my books are balanced, Lord" (*see* Luke 18:11, 12).

To understand true gratitude, we must first understand what a gift is. A gift is a symbol of love. We can't see love, so we use symbols, like a wedding ring. In giving us gifts, God is saying: "Here, I want you to have this. Enjoy it. See it as a symbol of my love for you." True gratitude is returning love for love.

Don't Be Afraid to Ask God for Things

Don't be embarrassed; ask for big things and little things. Ask for yourself and for others. Don't worry about asking for too much; it's impossible. With God there are no quotas, no items in short supply. Think big; ask for the large size. And don't be afraid to ask for "worldly" things. If it's important to you, God cares.

Of course, you know very well that you're not going to get everything you ask for. Some disappointments you'll take in stride, but some will really hurt. Sometimes at a later date you'll be able to look back and see why you were better off not getting what you asked for, but sometimes you may never see why—at least not in this life—and no amount of theology is ever going to explain why.

Share the Pain

When suffering comes, don't suffer in silence, and don't suffer alone. Don't try to handle life's setbacks all by yourself. Ask God to share the experience, to share the emotion with you. This goes specially for the crisis times when the roof falls in on you. At such critical moments, the academic statement that God can draw good from evil means nothing. Like a blind person, you can only cry out—perhaps not even in words—asking God to take your hand and lead you through.

(Thought: If God ever became a human being and experienced personal crises, wouldn't God be better able to share mine?)

Be Alert to God's Presence All Around You

Does nature's beauty move you? Do you like mountains, clouds, sun, and stars? These things are beautiful, and anyone can enjoy them. But when you encounter God, you see them as gifts. You see God in a flower, in a snowflake, in a blade of grass. You look at a sunset, and you see a personal gift from God who had you personally in mind. And then all the world becomes a church where heaven and earth proclaim the glory of God, who gives them to you.

Work with God

Even if your favorite daydream is an endless vacation, you know that you're going to work, and you want it that way. Why is this drive so basic? Because you're a lot like God, who is always busy, busy, busy evolving the universe and the human race as part of it. And your help is wanted. Not only are you called to evolve, but you're also called to play a role in helping God bring the world and the human race to completion. Compared to God's, our contribution is small, yet it's vital; it makes all the difference in the world. Because of that contribution, the universe is now *our* universe, and eventually it will become the masterpiece that we and God have produced together.

What does this mean for your daily life? It means that everything you do has a lasting effect. When you wash the dishes, clean the floor, ride the bus, do your homework, cut the grass, sew on a button, each of these has more than an immediate effect such as getting a house clean or collecting a salary. It also has a lasting effect on the big work, our work of evolution.

You may not be famous. Your picture may not be in the paper. But you are vital. When you sweep a floor, you and God sweep it together. When you finish, the two of you not only have a clean floor, but both of you have moved the universe a little way toward fulfillment.

Be with God

Church is not the only place you can meet and be with God. You can experience union with each other in any situation.

Encounterers like to get together with God, whom they meet everywhere. At the department store, at the factory, on the train, in front of the TV set—they keep bumping into God all over the place. They walk alone, and they bump into God. When they bump into other people, they bump into God.

People who encounter are sharers. Anything interesting or pleasant that happens to them, they share with God. Encounterers are also dumpers. Any problem at all, anything rotten that happens, they "dump" on God. They don't try to go it alone.

Encounterers are listeners. They listen to God everywhere. It's not that they expect phone calls from heaven, but they listen, and things do happen.

Encounterers like to get together with God. They like God's company. God feels the same way about them. And about you.

Remember, God Is Getting a Good Deal, Too

It's true that God, who is perfect, does not need us. And we know we are far from perfect. But if you are becoming an encounterer, then by this time you should not only love yourself but even like yourself. You know you have value, and you try to share this value by loving God.

Looking at you, God sees something beautiful and good. Why argue? God sees beyond your flaws and limitations to the interesting you, to the you who can and will be if you answer the call and stay close to the Lord and to others.

These are just a few helpful hints for you as you try to be with God and others. No two people encounter God in exactly the same way, and your relationship will be special, even unique. Eventually you may get comfortable with each other.

Things to Do

1. Can you describe any times in your life when you felt very much in touch with God?
2. Does the description of the cultural Christian reflect your own experience?
3. Have you ever been disappointed or angry with God? Did you express your feelings?

4. Would you describe your relationship with God as vertical or horizontal, both, or neither?
5. Are you able to find God in the ordinary events of daily life, or only in structured religious settings?

PART TWO

MEETINGS

7

First Friends

Talking about encountering God is much easier than actually doing it. Writing about a relationship with God is easier than cultivating one. Recall some of the obstacles that get in the way: inertia, fear, busyness, bad memories of past religious activities. Even if everything said so far had seemed reasonable and attainable, in practice we might find it very difficult to reach out to God.

We know from the experience of others that there are many ways of meeting the Lord: in nature, in people, in the pivotal events of our lives. But when they don't seem to happen to us, we begin to suspect that the problems lie not in God but in ourselves, and from deep within us there rises a cry for help.

God has heard our cry and has responded. It isn't up to us to make the encounter with God take place. We don't have to *make* it happen; we need only to *let* it happen. God has taken the initiative by becoming one of us in Jesus Christ. Christians know this in their heads, of course. Every Sunday at the Eucharist they profess their belief in the Incarnation when they recite the Creed. But has God-made-human ever touched their hearts? Have they, in personal, one-on-one fashion, ever met the Lord?

The account of the Last Supper in John's Gospel records an exchange between Jesus and one of his closest followers:

Philip said to him, "Master, show us the Father, and that will be enough for us." Jesus said to him, "Have I been with you for so long a time and you still do not know me, Philip? Whoever has seen me has seen the Father. How can you say, 'Show us the Father'?" — John 14:8-9

Philip was one of the inner circle of Jesus' disciples. For months and years he had been living in close intimacy with this man. They acknowledged him as their leader because they were convinced that he was God's spokesman, sent to reveal to them their Father who was in heaven. Being with him, watching him, and listening to him, they felt close to God in a very special way. Tonight they were troubled and sad, because he had just told them he must leave them and return to his Father. So Philip, speaking for the group, utters the same cry for help that we do: "Show us the Father! Help us to encounter the living God, here and now." He speaks for us, too, and for anyone who has ever yearned to see the face of God, who seems so absent, so remote.

Jesus answers both him and us: The way to God is through God's son. He is the best means for us to find ourselves, relate to one another in love, and achieve union with God. We come in contact with God through Jesus in many ways, but one special way is through the New Testament. The Gospel accounts of the life, death, and resurrection of Christ can put us in touch with him, for they are the very word of God addressed to each of us here and now.

When we read the Gospels in a spirit of faith and openness to God's word, we come in living contact with Jesus Christ, who reveals the Father to us and shares God's life with us. The Gospel accounts are not just stories about other people long ago and far away. They are about us and our lives, and are addressed to each of us in a very personal way. They can actually help us to meet the living God.

What you need is not just information about God or facts about Jesus. These have their place, but they are not the heart of the matter. To really know someone and to relate to him or her as a friend, you need to encounter people, to meet them on an interpersonal level. What we want, after all, is not to be experts on God, but to *know* God. Becoming a scripture scholar is nice, but becoming a Christian is better. Being a theologian has its advantages, but it's more important to be a person of faith, in touch with God and sharing God's life. A reflective and prayerful reading of the Gospels, watching what Jesus does and listening to what he says, is a tried and true way of getting in close personal touch with God.

In this part of the book, selected events in the life of Christ will be presented and commented on, but not with the purpose of exegesis and explanation. Rather, the purpose is to flesh out and enliven these events as encounter-causers for you, the twentieth- and twenty-first-century reader. The intention is not to transport you back in time to the first century, but rather to take a first-century event and bring it into the present, to help you discover and attain your basic heart wishes.

A possible obstacle to this outcome is what we call the Creprus Syndrome. To understand this ailment, which strikes so many cultural Christians, imagine a mythical island somewhere between Crete and Cyprus, called Creprus. As Paul sails on his second missionary journey, his notes are washed overboard and float ashore at Creprus. On his third missionary journey some years later, Paul lands at Creprus, comes into the nearest town, and begins, with enthusiasm, to tell the people the Good News of Christ. But all he gets from them is a big ho hum. "We know all those stories. We read them when they washed ashore a few years ago."

The Creprus Syndrome can happen to anyone who has grown up hearing the Jesus story over and over. Some people think they know the story but have never been part of it and have never let it happen to them. Maybe in the past you have studied a "life" of Christ and have been given a series of Gospel passages with a common theme plus an explanation.

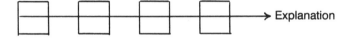

In this book, the approach is different. Many Gospel incidents are presented not so much to explain or tell a story as to lead you to an encounter with God. You can experience the Gospel not just as a history or as a book of religious information but as an encounter-causer. It's not necessary that each passage lead to such a meeting. Maybe only a few will.

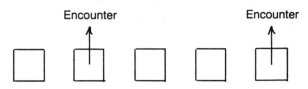

Even if only a few passages contribute to such an experience, your whole attitude toward the Gospels may change. They can be the occasion of personal religious experience and enlightenment. And even those passages which do not affect you this way now may do so later.

None of this can happen, of course, unless you are open to the experience. Don't say, "I've heard these stories before." Try again — and this time, try to get into the story.

Readers of the Gospels can sometimes be misled by their simplicity. The Gospels are similar to a powerful movie scene that calls for enormously detailed and lengthy preparation before the brief, swift shooting. The deceptively simple event is recorded, and the impact and implications are only gradually realized.

A poem of two hundred words is short indeed. Yet the total input of ideas, insights, and emotions that go to create the concise two hundred words is enormous. If these were all written out, the poem might come to many thousands of words. Because of this great input, a great amount may be drawn from the poem. The *haiku*, a poem that is only seventeen syllables long, is a striking example of this kind of literature.

The Gospels are a classic example of this type of concise medium. They are short, and at first glance seem to be a simple collection of brief episodes, homey examples, everyday occurrences. Yet, because of the input by the evangelists and faith of the community to whom they speak, there is enormous potential output.

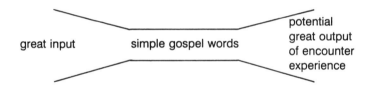

great input   simple gospel words   potential
great output
of encounter
experience

The apparently artless Gospel narratives are not meant to encompass knowledge like an encyclopedia, nor are they written in the style of the daily newspaper. Yet they transmit reality. A phone book reports information but does not make for exciting reading. A letter from a loved one is not as neat and tidy as a phone book but means a lot more.

The Gospels are like letters. The writers try to share an experience, their reaction to an event. Hence the Gospels have special characteristics. Their stylized format comes from a variety of sources composed over a long period of time. The presentation is many layered, the result of editorial work. Episodes, sometimes taken out of time sequence, are telescoped and interwoven. Post-Resurrection insights are inserted into earlier events. All of this is done to share a reality, not merely report it.

Recall, at the outset, what we said earlier about the importance of expanding one's heart wishes. Jesus' message is addressed to people who have more than a tunnel vision of what they want out of existence. Jesus cannot be seen or heard by those who are determined to live their lives within safe, narrow boundaries. Such people look into a limited future where all they need is themselves. To achieve these circumscribed goals, they need neither God nor other people. To them, the Gospel message is completely irrelevant.

When we break out of that tunnel and expand our heart wishes and what we want out of existence, we see that we cannot possibly attain these expanded heart wishes without help. Then we will be ready to hear the Gospel message.

Sometimes we need a crisis in order to be able to break out. Maybe life has been going along comfortably, but then comes a crisis. It may be sickness, loneliness, complete boredom, frustration, a feeling that there has to be more to life than this, a loss of some kind, a total religious disorientation—the list of possibilities is endless. At such a time we may hit bottom and feel completely helpless. All we can do is cry out and not know if anyone is listening.

Crises are no fun when we are going through them, but they can be a sign of encounter to come, perhaps an encounter in a Gospel context. This pattern seems observable in the ministry of Jesus of Nazareth. The people he touched were usually in a crisis situation, sometimes consciously, sometimes beneath the surface of awareness. Some were trying to cope with bereavement or sickness. Others were dissatisfied with themselves. Some were looking for broader horizons. These were the ones who were excited or inspired or who turned themselves around under his influence. The comfortable, the prosperous, the complacent, the self-satisfied never had a clue as to what he was about.

So try to approach each Gospel theme with a fresh, open mind and heart, as though you had never heard it before. Let's start the way two young friends of Jesus started, by being introduced to him. It was on the banks of the Jordan River, where a charismatic figure named John the Baptist was leading a religious revival. Come back in imagination to that far-off day, and meet the Lord.

FIRST FRIENDS

The next day John was there again with two of his disciples, and as he watched Jesus walk by, he said, "Behold, the Lamb of God." The two disciples heard what he said and followed Jesus. Jesus turned and saw them following him and said to them, "What are you looking for?" They said to him, "Rabbi" (which translated means Teacher), "where are you staying?" He said to them, "Come, and you will see." So they went and saw where he was staying, and they stayed with him that day. It was about four in the afternoon. Andrew, the brother of Simon Peter, was one of the two who heard John and followed Jesus. He first found his own brother Simon and told him, "We have found the Messiah" (which is translated Anointed). Then he brought him to Jesus. Jesus looked at him and said, "You are Simon the son of John; you will be called Kephas" (which is translated Peter).

The next day he decided to go to Galilee, and he found Philip. And Jesus said to him, "Follow me." Now Philip was from Bethsaida, the town of Andrew and Peter. Philip found Nathanael and told him, "We have found the one about whom Moses wrote in the law, and also the prophets, Jesus, son of Joseph, from Nazareth." — John 1:35-45

They were two young fishermen, caught up in the religious revival that centered around John the Baptist. They had no idea, the morning of that fateful day, that before the sun set, the whole direction of their lives would be changed. Even at the day's end, they still didn't realize what had happened to them. There was nothing dramatic or spectacular about their encounter with the young carpenter from Nazareth. It all happened so quietly, so unobtrusively: a chance meeting, an invitation to spend a few hours, a conversation that started tentatively and grew more earnest, and a promise to come again and bring some friends. John never dreamed that many, many years later, when he was a very old man, he would recall so clearly that they met at four o'clock in the afternoon.

He and Andrew always looked back on that evening as the turning point in their lives. Behind them was the world of other young men on fishing boats, looking forward to getting out on their own, marrying and raising a family, finding their place in the small, busy town on the lakeshore in Galilee. It was a safe, predictable, conventional world with few surprises. Ahead of them was an unbelievable series of events: the restless journeys crisscrossing Palestine, the unforgettable sermons, the signs and wonders, the shifting moods of the crowds, the violent end on the hill of crucifixion, and the explosion of new life with the risen Lord. And then would come their own ministries, the beginnings of the church, and the scattering abroad to conquer new worlds.

What a turnaround! And it all began with a brief encounter and a few hours together. What did they talk about that first day? What could have started such incredible events in motion?

Most likely it was a very ordinary conversation. It wasn't what they talked about, but the effect they had on one another. John and Andrew were idealistic young men, looking for something bigger than the small world that beckoned to them. That's what attracted them to the Baptist and brought them to the banks of the Jordan in the days of their youth. So when the prophet pointed out Jesus to them, they followed, timidly at first, and at a distance. That was when the stranger turned around.

"What are you looking for?"

What are we looking for? How can we answer that one, when we don't know ourselves? How can we put into words the emptiness, the longing for something bigger than we've ever known, something better than we've ever looked forward to? We'd feel foolish if we tried to express in words the desires that we can hardly name ourselves.

"Where are you staying?"

"Come, and you will see."

And that's how it all began — an attitude of openness on their part, a simple invitation accepted, a little time spent together. They didn't know it yet, but from that moment on, nothing would ever be the same again.

The remarkable thing about this story is that it still happens. Every day, people meet Jesus Christ and, by their own admission, are changed. They are convinced that in meeting Christ, they are coming in touch with the living God who transforms them by grace and opens up horizons they never dreamed of. They are poor people and rich people, struggling people and successful people, scholars and illiterates and in between. They are women and men, old and young, of every race and nationality, and they all agree on one thing: It can happen to you, too. All you need is to be open, to accept an invitation, to spend a little time together ... and be willing to go wherever he leads. Pry open the lid on your heart, expand your desires, and make yourself available for a new world of experience. Start with the simple question: "Where do you live?" and be willing to come and see.

We are going to tell, once again, the story of Jesus and the people in his life. We invite you to share it, not as a spectator watching other people from another time and place, but as one of the characters in a real-life drama that is unfolding right now, which you and God can write together.

We're not simply going to retell the story the way you have heard it many times before. Rather, we will dwell on several incidents in the Gospel narrative when Jesus encounters other people, to see how they affect one another, and what happens to them. And we'll try to see if we are in the story, too.

We are convinced that God became human in Jesus Christ in order to encounter you and me and to establish love relationships between us. We believe that a prayerful study of Jesus' encounters with people can help us meet God in him and in one another. We are convinced that God's word has this power, that God's grace is available to us if we but open ourselves to it. If you have trouble relating to a far-off, distant, faceless God, then join us and draw near to him who first loved us. He has a question for you: What are you looking for? And if you want to know where he lives, come and see.

If you're not too rushed and are willing to spend a few hours with the Son of God, you can meet him in a very personal way. He won't force himself on you, but if you take the risk that goes with any human encounter, there's no telling where it may lead. For John and Andrew it was a small beginning that led to greatness.

Things to Do

1. Have the Gospels ever affected you in a very personal way? What was the passage, and what did it do for you?
2. Have you ever been afflicted with the Creprus Syndrome?
3. In your opinion, what was it about Jesus that attracted these young men and drew them to him?
4. When John and Andrew decided to follow Jesus instead of pursuing their careers as fishermen, do you think their parents and neighbors all approved? Do you see young people acting this way today?
5. Do you see anything of yourself in this story?
6. What are *you* looking for?

8

Taking Sides

That first encounter between Jesus and his friends was the beginning of his public ministry. The next couple of years were filled with other meetings, with signs and wonders. He taught the people, healed their sicknesses of body and soul, and gained an enthusiastic following. He also made enemies, as the leaders of the religious establishment came to regard him as a threat to their positions. As it turned out, his enemies were more determined and better organized than his friends, but more of that later.

His ministry was mostly in Galilee, in northern Palestine, and occasionally in Jerusalem, the political and religious capital of the nation. During those years he met all kinds of people who reacted to him and his message in an extraordinary variety of ways. Gradually it became clear what was happening: People were choosing up sides, either for him or against him. The stakes were high, and the game was for keeps.

In the next few chapters we will meet some of the people whose paths crossed that of Jesus of Nazareth and whose lives were decisively affected by that meeting.

In this chapter we will look closely at three encounters:

• an unplanned fishing trip
• a secret night meeting with a religious leader
• a crowd with a craving for food but not for faith

As you watch these people meet Christ, you may also encounter him in a new way. And don't be surprised if you meet yourself, too.

A MARVELOUS CATCH

Once while Jesus was standing beside the lake of Gennesaret, and the crowd was pressing in on him to hear the word of God, he saw two boats there at the shore of the lake; the fishermen had gone out of them and were washing their nets. He got into one of the boats, the one belonging to Simon, and asked him to put out a little way from the shore. Then he sat down and taught the crowds from the boat. When he had finished speaking, he said to Simon, "Put out into the deep water and let down your nets for a catch." Simon said, "Master, we have worked all night long but have caught nothing. Yet if you say so, I will let down the nets." When they had done this, they caught so many fish that their nets were beginning to break. So they signaled their partners in the other boat to come and help them. And they came and filled both boats, so that they began to sink. But when Simon Peter saw it, he fell down at Jesus' knees, saying, "Go away from me, Lord, for I am a sinful man." For he and all who were with him were amazed at the catch of fish that they had taken; and so also were James and John, sons of Zebedee, who were partners with Simon. Then Jesus said to Simon, "Do not be afraid; from now on you will be catching people." When they had brought their boats to shore, they left everything and followed him.—Luke 5:1-11 (New Revised Standard Version)

There's nothing unusual about finding a beach too crowded, but this was different. Everyone was pushing and shoving for the best places to hear a charismatic young preacher. It was a rock concert promoter's dream—a sellout, with even standing room hard to find. That was how Jesus, early in his public life, affected people. Without promotion, without gimmicks, simply through the quiet power of his fascinating personality, he drew them. And he held them with nothing but words.

The words were deceptively simple. He told stories drawn from the everyday world of farmers, shopkeepers, and housewives. In language that the least educated could understand, he told them about their lives and about the care and the plans that God had for them.

As they listened, they felt better about themselves and closer to God. That's why they were here on the lakeshore today, instead of cleaning the house or minding the store. They didn't want to miss a word.

Jesus didn't want to disappoint them, so he had a good idea. Simon Peter, one of the young fishermen who was between trips, had beached his boat. He used to spend much of his spare time with a small group who had attached themselves informally to Jesus, so he was somewhat flattered and eager to help when the young preacher asked to use his boat for a pulpit. Now the people couldn't crowd around too close without getting their feet wet, and Jesus had a good spot from which to address them.

Peter felt good when the talk was over; he was glad he had been able to help. For a while, listening to Jesus, he had forgotten the disappointment of the previous night's fishing trip. Hours of backbreaking work, rowing and casting and hauling, had turned up nothing. *Well, maybe tonight will be better. Meanwhile it's good to rest and listen to my new friend.*

So he was quite taken aback when Jesus made his unexpected suggestion: "While we're out here in the water, let's drop the nets and catch some fish."

How do you like that? He's a good carpenter and a great preacher, but he doesn't know anything about fishing. It's the wrong time and the wrong place; we found that out last night. Better to wait for dark and try a different location. And the men are tired. Why not quit while we're behind?

All these thoughts came to Peter's mind, and they were almost on his lips when something made him pause. There was something about the way Jesus made the request, something in his manner that made Peter reconsider. *He knows what I'm thinking, but he wants me to trust him. The practical, down-to-earth realist in me says "Forget it!" The other side of me—the dreamer, the adventurer—says "Why not? You never can tell what may happen!"*

So Simon Peter trusted Jesus and took a chance. He and his men rowed into deep water and let down the nets. Have you ever seen the fishing nets used on the Sea of Galilee? They're big and clumsy, and a sweep with them takes a lot of hard work. The men were tired from a fruitless night's fishing, and they had no realistic hope of scoring this time. But Jesus was a hard man to say no to, and some instinct stronger than prudence led them on.

What a shock when the school of fish struck the nets! For a while, as they dragged the catch into the boat and frantically signaled the men in the other boat to help, they were too busy even to be amazed. But when it was all over and they had beached the boats and unloaded their tremendous catch, a profound sense of awe took hold of them. Now it dawned on them that they were in the presence of some mysterious power beyond their experience or comprehension. Peter was the first to put this feeling into words. "Go away from me, Lord! I am a sinful man!" In the presence of the holy and the sacred, he was painfully aware of his faults. Maybe if he were perfect he'd feel at home with Jesus; as it was, the gulf between them was too much to bear.

This is the way people often feel about God. They'd rather wait until they're perfect before they try to get close. Overwhelmed by their own shortcomings, they can't imagine God wanting to have anything to do with them.

To Peter, and to every person who has ever felt this way, Jesus has a simple, reassuring answer: "Don't be afraid." This spectacular catch of fish is just a sign pointing to something much greater. Someday soon they will win the minds and hearts of men and women and bring them to Christ. That will be the real miracle – not a net bulging with fish, but the triumph of God's grace in people's hearts through the ministry of imperfect, sinful human beings.

At that moment, Peter and John and Andrew and the others knew what they had been looking for, and that they had found it. "They left everything and followed Jesus."

Jesus worked a miracle that day because Peter let him. Peter trusted Jesus and took a chance. If he hadn't opened himself up to the new experiences available in that encounter, nothing would have happened. All sorts of possibilities in him might never have been realized, and history would long since have forgotten—indeed, never known—about a few Galilean fishermen in an obscure town. An invitation from Christ and the acceptance of the invitation in the spirit of trust and adventure made all the difference.

Could the same thing happen to you? Well, why do you suppose he did it? For the fish?

A MEETING AT NIGHT

Now there was a Pharisee named Nicodemus, a ruler of the Jews. He came to Jesus at night and said to him, "Rabbi, we know that you are a teacher who has come from God, for no one can do these signs that you are doing unless God is with him." Jesus answered and said to him, "Amen, amen, I say to you, no one can see the kingdom of God without being born from above." Nicodemus said to him, "How can a person once grown old be born again? Surely he cannot reenter his mother's womb and be born again, can he?" Jesus answered, "Amen, amen, I say to you, no one can enter the kingdom of God without being born of water and Spirit. What is born of flesh is flesh and what is born of spirit is spirit. Do not be amazed that I told you, 'You must be born from above.' The wind blows where it wills, and you can hear the sound it makes, but you do not know where it comes from or where it goes; so it is with everyone who is born of the Spirit."

For God so loved the world that he gave his only Son, so that everyone who believes in him might not perish but might have eternal life.—John 3:1-8, 16

One of the striking things about Jesus and the way he related to people was his ability to adapt to them. With farmers and fishermen and merchants, he spoke in simple, picturesque terms, using stories and examples taken from their workaday world. With learned religious leaders like Nicodemus, he could speak the subtle language of rabbinical theology. He met people where they were, but he didn't leave them there. While accepting them for the persons they were, he challenged them to go further— to broaden their horizons and break out of the narrow, comfortable world in which they might become stagnant.

Nicodemus was trying to play both sides of the street. As a member of the Sanhedrin, he associated with men who were bitter enemies of Christ. Yet he had been deeply impressed by the young prophet and wanted to be his disciple. The only way he could do this, without surrendering his influential position on the Council, was to visit Jesus secretly at night. Jesus accepted him on these terms; he didn't insist on a decision, at least not just now. Indeed, he made himself available and helped Nicodemus find his own way in his own good time.

But he doesn't let Nicodemus stand still, either. He shakes him up with the mysterious assertion that if he wishes to be a success, he must be born again. Nicodemus doesn't know what Jesus means, so he pretends to take him literally: "How can a grown man be born again?" But Jesus pushes on. Instead of explaining, he gets in deeper. "You must be born again of water and the Spirit." Here Jesus is challenging Nicodemus to go beyond the clever games of the learned and plunge into mysteries too deep to be understood. He is saying, in effect, "Nicodemus, I don't care how clever or learned you are. There are things both in nature and in the world of the spirit that you will never fully understand. Just because you don't fully understand them doesn't mean that they are any less real."

Many people think that mysteries are something found only in religion, but they are all around us. For example, take the wind. As Jesus points out to Nicodemus, we cannot see the wind (though we can hear it). We don't know where it comes from or where it goes. But even though we don't understand it, we still believe in it. If we didn't, things would get blown away, sometimes even ourselves. We don't understand electricity, either, or a thousand things revealed to us under the scientist's microscope. And we don't fully understand people, who are perhaps the most mysterious of all, because they're like God.

In speaking to Nicodemus, Jesus is addressing those educated, cultured people who like their universe served up logical and intellectually respectable. These are the sophisticates who are embarrassed and uncomfortable with mystery because it looks too much like superstition. He tells them (us?) that the search for God calls for much more than brains. It calls for trust, for a willingness to accept truths our minds cannot comprehend.

Does this present a problem? Of course it does. An intelligent person tries to develop a critical mind. This is wise, because every day all kinds of people try to make us believe all kinds of nonsense, and not just in television commercials, either. But the kind of faith we're talking about, the faith that Jesus wants, isn't the same as being gullible. He doesn't so much ask us to believe *things* as to believe *him.* When Nicodemus said, "We know you are a teacher sent from God," that was a statement of faith. It meant he was ready to be led further, to go deeper into the mystery of life in God. So Jesus lets him in on the great secret he had come to reveal: We are all meant to be born again in Baptism, that a new and wonderful life is there waiting for us, if we choose to accept it.

Once we believe in Jesus Christ, a whole new world can open up for us. Like Nicodemus, we'll be asked to believe things, just on his word, that sound almost too good to be true, things such as: "God so loved the world that he gave his only Son, so that everyone who believes in him might not perish but might have eternal life."

THE BREAD OF LIFE

After this, Jesus went across the Sea of Galilee. A large crowd followed him, because they saw the signs he was performing on the sick. Jesus went up on the mountain, and there he sat down with his disciples. The Jewish feast of Passover was near. When Jesus raised his eyes and saw that a large crowd was coming to him, he said to Philip, "Where can we buy enough food for them to eat?" He said this to test him, because he himself knew what he was going to do. Philip answered him, "Two hundred days' wages worth of food would not be enough for each of them to have a little [bit]." One of the disciples, Andrew, the brother of Simon Peter, said to him, "There is a boy here who has five barley loaves and two fish; but what good are these for so many?" Jesus said, "Have the people recline." Now there was a great deal of grass in that place. So the men reclined, about five thousand in number. Then Jesus took the loaves, gave thanks, and distributed them to those who were reclining, and also as much of the fish as they wanted. When they had had their fill, he said to his disciples, "Gather the fragments left over, so that nothing will be wasted." So they collected them, and filled twelve wicker baskets with fragments from the five barley loaves that had been more than they could eat. — John 6:1-13

Next Day

And when they found him across the sea they said to him, "Rabbi, when did you get here?" Jesus answered them and said, "Amen, amen, I say to you, you are looking for me not because you saw signs but because you ate the loaves and were filled. Do not work for food that perishes but for the food that endures for eternal life, which the Son of Man will give you. For on him the Father, God, has set his seal."

"For the bread of God is that which comes down from heaven and gives life to the world."

So they said to him, "Sir, give us this bread always." Jesus said to them, "I am the bread of life; whoever comes to me will never hunger, and whoever believes in me will never thirst."

"I am the living bread that came down from heaven; whoever eats this bread will live forever; and the bread that I will give is my flesh for the life of the world."

The Jews quarreled among themselves, saying, "How can this man give us [his] flesh to eat?" Jesus said to them, "Amen, amen, I say to you, unless you eat the flesh of the Son of Man and drink his blood, you do not have life within you. Whoever eats my flesh and drinks my blood has eternal life, and I will raise him on the last day. For my flesh is true food, and my blood is true drink. Whoever eats my flesh and drinks my blood remains in me and I in him."

Then many of his disciples who were listening said, "This saying is hard; who can accept it?"

As a result of this, many [of] his disciples returned to their former way of life and no longer accompanied him.

Jesus then said to the Twelve, "Do you also want to leave?" Simon Peter answered him, "Master, to whom shall we go? You have the words of eternal life. We have come to believe and are convinced that you are the Holy One of God." — John 6:25-27, 33-35, 51-56, 60, 66-69

When people visit the lakeshore area where Jesus fed the crowd with the loaves and fish, the question hits them right away: What was the problem? They weren't very far from nearby towns. If he had sent them away to find a late supper for themselves, it would have been an inconvenience, nothing more. The miracle was unnecessary; was it performed, then, just for show? No, certainly not that. Jesus never used his power merely to astound or impress, but only to serve people's needs. Why, then, did they need this miracle? Not because they needed bread, but because they needed a sign.

When we love someone very much, we want to give that person not just presents or words or even deeds. We want to give ourselves. In this we are like God, who was not content to send prophets or save the people from afar, but went all the way and became one of us in Jesus Christ. But Jesus didn't even stop there. He wanted to be with us always, in the closest, most intimate union possible. He would give us his own flesh and blood to eat and drink, in the Eucharist. But first he had to prepare us for this gift through a sign.

The preparation had begun a long, long time before. Almost thirteen centuries earlier, the Hebrews had found themselves short of food as their nomadic wanderings took them through a desert place. At that time they unexpectedly came upon a strange new kind of food that saved them from starvation. Seeing God's hand in this saving event, they called the food manna — bread from heaven. It was this event that the people may have remembered when Jesus fed them with the loaves and fish, and of which he will remind them when he promises the Eucharist.

When they came to him in great numbers in the synagogue the next day, he wasted no time in getting to the point. He was almost harsh in his bluntness. "You've come to me because yesterday I gave you a free meal. You received food for nothing, and that impressed you. Look beyond the bread; it's only a sign.

Expand your heart wishes. Widen your perspective. I have much greater things to give you."

Step by step he led them on. "Don't work for perishable food, but for food that remains unto life eternal, food which I will give you."

They were eager now, and attentive. "Sir, give us this bread always."

And then he told them what he had been leading up to: "I am the bread of life." He himself was to be their food and drink. His own flesh and blood would be their pledge of everlasting life.

That was when the prudent, sensible, calculating people took over. "What's that? His flesh and blood? How can he do that?" And the spell was broken. Pedestrian minds took over and brought everyone down to earth. "Come, now, let's be reasonable. This is just too much to believe. You're not serious, are you?"

If being popular was important to Jesus, it was clear what he should have done at that moment. If he didn't want to lose the crowd, he should have said something like this: "Well, now, hold on. Let's talk this over. I think we have a breakdown in communication here. Maybe you folks are taking me too literally. I didn't say you'll actually eat my flesh and drink my blood. No, I meant it like sort of a symbol. You know, like when you eat the bread and drink the wine, you'd be reminded of me. A kind of memorial supper, if you know what I mean."

That's what he would have said if public relations had been his strong suit. Instead, he spelled it out and nailed it down: "Amen, amen, I say to you, unless you eat the flesh of the Son of Man and drink his blood, you do not have life within you. For my flesh is true food, and my blood is true drink."

That did it. The crowd broke up, and most of them never came back. They had eaten the loaves Christ multiplied the day before, but still they left. Jesus' Nielsen rating was never quite so high again. Instead of telling people what they wanted to hear, he told them the truth. If they trusted him, then maybe at a later time he could explain. If they didn't trust him now, no matter how much of an explanation he gave, it wouldn't make a bit of difference.

This was the moment of truth, the moment of trust, the moment of the "leap," the adventure.

Many refused the trust, the "leap," the adventure, and went away. Christ, discouraged, turned to the Twelve and asked, "You, too. Are you going to go away?"

There was an awkward silence, and then Peter answered for the others. "Look, Lord, I'm terribly confused. I don't understand this at all. At the moment I don't know what this talk was all about. But I trust you. I've been with you now for some time. I know you've got it. I know you are from heaven. If we leave you, where are we going to go?"

Peter didn't understand the Eucharist any better than the crowd did. It was just as mind-boggling for him. So what did he do? His trust in Jesus overcame the darkness and confusion of his mind. Instead of playing it safe, he took the leap of faith and brought the eleven with him.

He can take you with him, too. All you have to do is say the words, "Lord, to whom shall we go? You have the words of eternal life." Say the words, and mean them.

Things to Do

1. If Peter and the others had been prudent and sensible and left the nets out to dry, how would that have changed their lives?
2. Did you ever take a chance against your better judgment? What happened?
3. Do most people think of following Christ as a form of risk taking? Do you?
4. What does "being born again" mean to you?
5. Is it more difficult for intelligent and educated people to be religious?
6. "Christians believe not in some*thing* but in some*one*." Explain.
7. Does the miraculous feeding on the hillside and Jesus' discourse in the synagogue help you appreciate the Eucharist?
8. One evening the crowd wanted to make him king; the next day they deserted him. How did Jesus' stock go up so fast

and come down so fast? What does this tell you about him and them?

9. Did the apostles who stayed understand Jesus' promise any more than the crowd that left? Why did they stay?

9

Turning It Around

Perhaps the most striking characteristic of Jesus that emerges from a careful reading of the Gospels was the varying impact he had on the different people he met. It ranged all the way from the superficial to the profound. He could inspire passionate loyalty, and he could provoke murderous enmity.

Sometimes the effect was negligible, as in the case of the crowds. These came out of curiosity, were briefly impressed or astounded, but soon wandered off. They never really encountered him or got beneath the surface of who he was and what he was doing. They were mere observers, not participants in his story. Those who were sick and hurting found in him comfort and strength. Idealists were attracted to him as a leader and an inspiration. The powerful and the comfortable and the hypocrites saw in him a dangerous fanatic who had to be eliminated.

The most important determinant of people's reaction to Jesus was what they brought to the meeting. The crowd brought little and derived less. The sick had no illusions about themselves. They knew they needed help, they asked for it, and they received it. The idealists brought their expanded heart wishes and came away on fire with zeal. His enemies closed their minds and hearts and were the worse for having met him.

Two people depicted in the Gospels responded to him in an extraordinary way. One was a corrupt tax collector, the other a woman of easy virtue. Reading their stories, we get a glimpse of what a difference Jesus can make in our lives.

UP A TREE

He came to Jericho and intended to pass through the town. Now a man there named Zacchaeus, who was a chief tax collector and also a wealthy man, was seeking to see who Jesus was; but he could not see him because of the crowd, for he was short in stature. So he ran ahead and climbed a sycamore tree in order to see Jesus, who was about to pass that way. When he reached the place, Jesus looked up and said to him, "Zacchaeus, come down quickly, for today I must stay at your house." And he came down quickly and received him with joy. When they all saw this, they began to grumble, saying, "He has gone to stay at the house of a sinner." But Zacchaeus stood there and said to the Lord, "Behold, half of my possessions, Lord, I shall give to the poor, and if I have extorted anything from anyone, I shall pay it four times over." And Jesus said to him, "Today salvation has come to this house because this man too is a descendant of Abraham. For the Son of Man has come to seek and to save what was lost." — Luke 19:1-10

Sometimes we imagine that traveling with Jesus was like moving around in a portable church — very solemn, with everybody standing around praying or looking up to heaven or at least very serious. With Jesus making profound statements and the apostles checking their notes to make sure they got it down right. ("Did you get that one about turning the other cheek?")

Of course it wasn't that way at all. Sometimes people did the most unexpected things, like taking a roof apart to let a sick man down where Jesus could cure him. Then there was the tax collector who climbed the tree. His name was Zacchaeus. In Jericho he was nobody's favorite person, because he made his living collecting taxes for the Romans. Anybody who worked for the hated Romans, an occupying power, was looked down on, but a tax collector was the lowest form of life. He was not your basic IRS person, who does what most people consider an honest, respectable job. The tax-gathering system in the Roman Empire was shot through with corruption from top to bottom.

Even if the Romans had not been hated as a pagan occupying force, their tax collectors would have been despised, and usually on merit.

So the day that Jesus passed through Jericho, Zacchaeus had a problem. As usual, there was a big crowd, and the pushing and shoving made it hard to get a good spot where you could see him. It was doubly difficult for a man like Zacchaeus, who was not only unpopular but also short. Other little guys could get to the front because people could see over them, but nobody was going to let that rotten little grafter through. So what could he do? So climb a tree.

It wasn't the most dignified thing he could have done. Nobody looks twice when a child climbs a tree, but the local IRS man? Well, this was no ordinary day for Zacchaeus. Something about the arrival of the young preacher from Galilee had him all excited. What was it that made him climb that tree? Was it just curiosity? Or was there a feeling of urgency that he could sense but not define? From what happened later, we can guess that Zacchaeus wasn't happy with his life, that he was looking for something he couldn't name. Maybe he had a secret ambition to be an honest man. Maybe he just wanted to stop being a social outcast and have some friends besides other tax collectors. Whatever it was, the appearance of Jesus brought it to a head. He just had to get a look at him. If you asked him why, he couldn't have told you.

Well, you know what happened. He not only got to see Jesus, he met him and talked with him. First there was that unforgettable moment when Jesus looked up into the branches of the sycamore tree and saw him. There have been some silly debates over the years about whether Jesus ever laughed. If he didn't laugh at that moment, he certainly must have cracked a great big smile. Nobody else was smiling; seeing Zacchaeus was enough to spoil anybody's day.

Then Jesus made one of those totally unexpected gestures that were his trademark. He didn't just greet Zacchaeus and draw attention to him. He invited himself to dinner! You must understand that in that social situation, that was the greatest honor that Jesus could have given Zacchaeus. And it was accepted as such. It delighted Zacchaeus and infuriated his enemies. If there was one sure way to lose popularity with the respectable townspeople, this was it.

But there was more to Jesus' behavior than met the eye. He wasn't just making a flamboyant, unconventional gesture to shake up the placid burghers of Jericho. In a most improbable way, he was encountering Zacchaeus. This was no mere social meeting; there was a chemistry between the two men that was volatile and potentially explosive, for Jesus sensed why Zacchaeus had climbed that tree and what he was really looking for. For a moment, there was no jostling crowd, no eager disciples, no hostile bystanders. There were only the two of them, and for one it was the turning point of his life.

Up till now, Jesus had all the good lines in the drama. He had taken the initiative, met Zacchaeus more than halfway, and responded generously to the other's timid overture. Now it was Zacchaeus's turn. He saw the resentment in his neighbors' eyes, heard their muttered complaints. How could he show them — and himself — that Jesus hadn't made a mistake? The answer was simple, but he was as amazed as they were to hear it coming from his own lips. "If I have cheated anyone, I will pay him back four times as much." (*Wow! Did I say that?*)

He said it, all right, and he must have meant it, for Jesus said that salvation came to Zacchaeus's house that day. There are a few things worth noting here. First, Zacchaeus must have done more than his share of cheating; otherwise his pledge to make restitution would have made no sense. Secondly, he must have been feeling guilty long before he ever climbed that tree; his conversion could hardly have happened so instantaneously. Finally, he had a lot of changes to make in his style of living and his relationships with others. It wouldn't be easy to go to the people who hated him and return their money.

Yes, Zacchaeus might have trouble adjusting to his new way of life. On the other hand, he could now live with himself. He felt like a new man. He would show his neighbors that his conversion was no mere flash in the pan. He still had to prove himself, but he felt that now he could. He had said it in front of Jesus, so there was no turning back.

You might say that Zacchaeus went out on a limb that day. He came down that tree a changed man. Jesus affected people that way. He perceives possibilities in us that no one else—not even ourselves—can. He makes the first move to encounter us, and if we're brave enough to respond, we can be changed for the better. It's scary, but if we can believe in ourselves half as much as he does, it's easy—almost as easy as falling out of a tree.

THE WOMAN AT THE WELL

[Jesus] had to pass through Samaria. So he came to a town of Samaria called Sychar, near the plot of land that Jacob had given to his son Joseph. Jacob's well was there. Jesus, tired from his journey, sat down there at the well. It was about noon.

A woman of Samaria came to draw water. Jesus said to her, "Give me a drink." His disciples had gone into the town to buy food. The Samaritan woman said to him, "How can you, a Jew, ask me, a Samaritan woman, for a drink?" (For Jews use nothing in common with Samaritans.) Jesus answered and said to her, "If you knew the gift of God and who is saying to you, 'Give me a drink,' you would have asked him and he would have given you living water."

[The woman] said to him, "Sir, you do not even have a bucket and the cistern is deep; where then can you get this living water? Are you greater than our father Jacob, who gave us this cistern and drank from it himself with his children and his flocks?" Jesus answered and said to her, "Everyone who drinks this water will be thirsty again; but whoever drinks the water I shall give will never thirst; the water I shall give will become in him a spring of water welling up to eternal life." The woman said to him, "Sir, give me this water, so that I may not be thirsty or have to keep coming here to draw water."

Jesus said to her, "Go call your husband and come back." The woman answered and said to him, "I do not have a husband." Jesus answered her, "You are right in saying, 'I do not have a husband.' For you have had five husbands, and the one you have now is not your husband. What you have said is true." The woman said to him, "Sir,

I can see that you are a prophet. Our ancestors worshiped on this mountain, but you people say that the place to worship is in Jerusalem." Jesus said to her, "Believe me, woman, the hour is coming when you will worship the Father neither on this mountain nor in Jerusalem. You people worship what you do not understand; we worship what we understand, because salvation is from the Jews. But the hour is coming, and is now here, when true worshipers will worship the Father in Spirit and truth; and indeed the Father seeks such people to worship him. God is Spirit, and those who worship him must worship in Spirit and truth." The woman said to him, "I know that the Messiah is coming, the one called the Anointed; when he comes, he will tell us everything." Jesus said to her, "I am he, the one who is speaking with you."

At that moment his disciples returned, and were amazed that he was talking with a woman, but still no one said, "What are you looking for?" or "Why are you talking with her?" The woman left her water jar and went into the town and said to the people, "Come see a man who told me everything I have done. Could he possibly be the Messiah?" They went out of the town and came to him.

Many of the Samaritans of that town began to believe in him because of the word of the woman who testified, "He told me everything I have done." When the Samaritans came to him, they invited him to stay with them; and he stayed there two days. Many more began to believe in him because of his word, and they said to the woman, "We no longer believe because of your word; for we have heard for ourselves, and we know that this is truly the savior of the world." — John 4:4-30, 39-42

You can still get a drink from Jacob's well today. Just enter the charming little Greek Orthodox chapel that's built over the well and ask the priest to draw a cupful for you; he's very obliging. It's pure and fresh and delicious the way tap water could never be. When Jesus stopped there, of course, there was no chapel. The noonday sun was merciless, and he was probably very thirsty. But he was looking for something more than water when he asked the Samaritan woman for a drink.

She must have wondered what he was after. She was used to men asking her for favors; was this another one? After all she had seen, it was pretty hard to shake her up; there weren't many surprises left for her. Even so, she didn't expect a Jew to talk to her. There was so much bad feeling between Samaritans and Jews in those days that they avoided one another as much as possible and frowned on all social contact. Jews passing through Samaria usually traveled in large groups, seeking safety in numbers. This woman, who had broken most of the taboos in her society, was still wary when Jesus broke this one. "How can you, a Jew, ask me, a Samaritan woman, for a drink?"

The way he answers makes her even more curious. If she knew who he was, he says, she would have asked him for living water, and he would have given it to her. Is he serious? Or is he another fast talker with a smooth line? (She knows all about *that* kind.) So she plays it straight and goes along with him. "You do not even have a bucket. How would you get it?" But instead of clearing up this strange little conversation, he gets even more mysterious. "Everyone who drinks this water will be thirsty again; but whoever drinks the water I shall give will never thirst."

He's talking in riddles. And she wonders, *Is he putting me on?* But there is something about him that makes her pause. He's not like the other men she's known. This one looks honest, and there's a quiet strength about him. *I feel as though I have to take him seriously, because—well, he takes me seriously.* So, instead of a wisecrack, she's surprised to hear herself say, "Sir, give me this water."

His reply is disconcerting. "Go call your husband and come back." And when she replies that she has no husband, he makes the most astounding statement yet: "You are right in saying, 'I do not have a husband.' For you have had five husbands, and the one you have now is not your husband."

Now that was sneaky! So that's what he was leading up to. Who is this stranger, anyway? And why am I letting him talk to me this way?

But she doesn't turn him off. Instead, she tries to change the subject. *Let's talk about religion; it's a lot less threatening subject than my love life. How about the long-standing dispute about the*

Temple? The Jews say it belongs in Jerusalem where it is; we Samaritans say it should be on this mountain.

Jesus goes along with her, more or less. He'll talk religion, but he makes it clear that the question of worshiping God is a lot bigger than Jerusalem or Samaria and that very soon this intramural argument will be obsolete. Does he mean the Messianic age is near, as many Jews and Samaritans hope? The Messiah, she says, will teach us these things. And she can hardly believe her ears when he comes up with one last bombshell: "I am he."

If anyone else had said that, she would have laughed and called him crazy. But this man isn't crazy, and he's not one to be laughed at.

What a time for his disciples to come back! There was so much she wanted to ask him, but she couldn't talk while they were there. So she ran back into town, even forgetting the water she had come for, and told everybody she met about the remarkable stranger. You can't help wondering why anyone paid any attention to her. She wasn't a respectable person. Many must have looked down on her for her bohemian life-style. She wasn't much different from a prostitute. If there's going to be a religious happening, they don't expect it from her.

And yet there was something about her that made them stop and listen and then want to see for themselves. She looked different today; she had had an experience that transformed her, even in the eyes of her friends and neighbors.

"He told me everything I have ever done." That's the expression that occurs more than once in this unusual conversion story. It stayed with her long after she'd forgotten what they'd said about temples and worship and theology. He had known all about her, or rather, he knew *her.* And in telling her what he knew about her, a strange thing happened: She came to see herself the way she never had before. For years she had been hiding from herself. She had gone from one man to another so quickly and easily that sometimes their names and faces got mixed up in her mind. Worse still, she was getting fuzzy about who *she* was—until this man spoke to her today.

"He told me everything I have ever done." Didn't she know what she had done? Why did she need him to tell her? Because sin is alienation. To be a sinner is to lose touch with our real selves, to accept the roles thrust upon us by others, to live up to other people's expectations instead of our own ideals, to surrender our values in exchange for some glittering bauble that shines in our eyes and blinds us to what is good and true. She had a lot of practice in covering up the truth from herself. She hadn't really looked in a mirror for years, until he made her do it. When he did, she didn't like what she saw, but somehow he made it bearable. Others had told her off before, in plain, blunt terms, but this wasn't just another put-down. He seemed to really care about her, and he gave her the feeling that she could be different. Was it because he believed in her more than she believed in herself?

People who get involved with Jesus Christ often have the same basic experience as the Samaritan woman. When I study him, listen to his words, and take them to heart, I find myself living at a different level of awareness. I get beyond the noise and beneath the surface, to the real me. It's like when he traveled through Galilee and Judea: When he was around, the masks came off, and those who wanted to keep their masks on stayed away. To some, the masks were so important that they would stop at nothing to keep them, even if it meant killing him.

Most people aren't anxious to know themselves the way God knows them. Most would rather live on the surface and settle for blurred, fuzzy images of themselves. It's safer that way. If I never really know myself, I'll never have to change anything. I can substitute routine for realization and avoid all the sweat that goes with being a real person.

Let's face it: When the Samaritan woman encountered Jesus and allowed him to get through to her, her life became complicated. Some things could never be the same again. She might have to give up some of her most cherished habits. Changes would have to be made. Where did she get the courage? From him, of course.

If you want to play it cozy and achieve the goal of undisturbed mediocrity, don't get too involved with Christianity. A little surface religiosity is all right, but stay away from the deep stuff. Encounters with Jesus are dangerous. They can reveal us to ourselves and make us dissatisfied with compromise. They can infect us with idealism and lead us on to high and noble resolves. They can even damage the crust of selfishness that surrounds our hearts and protects us from sacrifice. What happened to the Samaritan woman could happen to us: We might start to live.

Things to Do

1. Zacchaeus made a big change in his life that day. What do you think turned him around?
2. When Zacchaeus told his wife and family what he had done, what do you think their reaction was? If he were your husband or father or brother, what would you tell him?
3. Do you think Zacchaeus really changed that much? What is he going to have to do to make his resolution stick?
4. In her encounter with Jesus, did the Samaritan woman learn more about God or about herself? Does this tell you anything about the nature of religious experience?
5. Until she met Jesus, what kept the woman's real self hidden from her? Why did she have to meet him to find herself?
6. Have you ever had an experience like hers?

10

The Last Journey

As the opposition hardened and the circle of Jesus' friends grew smaller, he saw the clouds gathering and knew the storm must break very soon. He was on a collision course with the religious authorities, with whom a decisive confrontation could no longer be avoided. The crowds, though still fascinated by Jesus and subject to occasional bursts of enthusiasm, were clearly too fickle and unreliable to be counted on in the crunch. He knew that if push came to shove, they would either desert him or turn on him.

This left his inner circle of followers, still loyal to him but hopelessly muddled about him and the true nature of his mission. In the face of his clear denials, they persisted in fantasizing about an imminent upheaval, a social and political revolution with him at the head and them close behind. The longer they lived on these illusions, the more total would be their downfall when disaster struck. The time had come for plain talk, and it began outside a little town called Caesarea Philippi.

WHO DO YOU SAY THAT I AM?

When Jesus went into the region of Caesarea Philippi he asked his disciples, "Who do people say that the Son of Man is?" They replied, "Some say John the Baptist, others Elijah, still others Jeremiah or one of the prophets." He said to them, "But who do you say that I am?" Simon Peter said in reply, "You are the Messiah, the Son of the living

God." Jesus said to him in reply, "Blessed are you, Simon son of Jonah. For flesh and blood has not revealed this to you, but my heavenly Father. And so I say to you, you are Peter, and upon this rock I will build my church, and the gates of the netherworld shall not prevail against it. I will give you the keys to the kingdom of heaven. Whatever you bind on earth shall be bound in heaven; and whatever you loose on earth shall be loosed in heaven." — Matthew 16:13-19

If there's a turning point in the public life of Christ, it's the conversation at Caesarea Philippi between Jesus and his closest followers. The disciples didn't know what Jesus knew — that he was about to launch his last drive on Jerusalem. This Passover celebration will be his last, for the price of confrontation with Judea's religious leaders will be his own death.

As he prepared for this final showdown, Jesus was painfully aware that his followers were in no way ready for the fatal struggle. All his efforts to educate them seemed to have failed. No matter how he tried to divert them, they persisted in thinking that they were to be at the cutting edge of some social or political revolution that would transform Jewish society. And the means of establishing that kingdom, Jesus' humiliation and murder, would be incomprehensible.

The time for teaching is running out. He must tell them, in brutally plain language, what's going to happen. But first he must elicit an act of faith in himself, to carry them through the darkest hours of failure and disillusionment.

Perhaps it was after a meal on the road, while they were all together resting before the next journey. Like a candidate asking the results of the latest poll, he asks them, "Who do people say that the Son of Man is?" This is not the important question, but it will do for starters. The answers come quickly. "Some say John the Baptist, others Elijah, still others Jeremiah or one of the prophets."

Now for the big one.

"What about *you?* Who do you say that I am?"

They looked at one another. Something in the way he asked the question told them that this was a serious moment. He was not asking for a routine report now. He wanted to know where they stood. Why were they following him? What was the basis for their relationship? What did he mean to them?

Simon Peter was the first to find words for the deep feelings that stirred within them. Speaking for them all, he made that magnificent profession of faith: "You are the Messiah, the Son of the living God."

A pregnant silence followed, as Jesus looked around the group. In each man's eyes he read the wordless message: Yes, that goes for me. They had made the leap of trust and staked all on him and his word. They didn't grasp what he was about, but they grasped who he was. That's all he could expect for now, but it was enough to build on.

"Blessed are you, Simon son of Jonah," answered Jesus. "For flesh and blood has not revealed this to you, but my heavenly Father."

To recognize Jesus for what he is and to make an act of faith in him takes more than brains or education. It takes a revelation from God. Simon received that revelation and responded in faith, not because he was smarter or a better person than others, but because he was open to Jesus and gave God's grace a chance. In a word, he was offered the gift of faith and didn't turn it down. And that made all the difference. It made him a new man, and Jesus underlines this by giving him a new name. "You are Peter, and upon this rock I will build my church."

Peter and the Eleven, who have made the leap of faith, are to be the foundation stones of the New Order.

In some ways it was a weak foundation. The Twelve were uneducated, without political power or influence, fuzzy and confused, even about what their own leader had in mind. But there were strong points, too. They were idealistic, they wanted to do great things, they wanted to serve. Most important of all, they were personally committed to Jesus Christ. They had acknowledged him as their leader and Savior and had freely chosen to follow him wherever he might lead. They had almost no appreciation of what was involved, and this was going to cost them dearly in the tragic weeks ahead, but this personal commitment was ultimately going to see them through.

One of the most striking things about Jesus is this feeling he creates in people that they must make a decision about him. In his lifetime, very few people were neutral on the subject of Jesus of Nazareth. Most were either for him or against him, and that was the way he wanted it. There have always been those who tried to study him at a distance and keep it theoretical, but it's difficult if you listen to him and take him seriously. If he were just another philosopher with a theory on what life is all about, it would be easier to avoid taking a stand. We could accept some of his ideas and reject others. But it wasn't a philosophy that he offered us; it was himself. He didn't force himself on people, but he provoked and challenged them to take a stand in his regard.

Many, especially in our day, have tried to picture Jesus as an uncomplicated humanist promoting a simple message of love and nonviolence, uninterested in questions of God or religion. He becomes the equal of Socrates or Buddha or Gandhi, but nothing more. For them, the question of Jesus' divine sonship is a distraction. If they're right, it's hard to understand why he aroused such extremes of loyalty and hatred, and even harder to figure out why he was killed. Time and time again, on almost every page of the New Testament, we find him asking, in one way or another, the question he put to the Twelve at Caesarea Philippi: Who do you say that I am? For those who believed in him, the possibilities were unlimited. For those who didn't, Jesus couldn't make much happen.

How about you? Who do *you* say that he is?

ON TO JERUSALEM

From that time on, Jesus began to show his disciples that he must go to Jerusalem and suffer greatly from the elders, the chief priests, and the scribes, and be killed and on the third day be raised. Then Peter took him aside and began to rebuke him, "God forbid, Lord! No such thing shall ever happen to you." He turned and said to Peter, "Get behind me, Satan! You are an obstacle to me. You are thinking not as God does, but as human beings do."

Then Jesus said to his disciples, "Whoever wishes to come after me must deny himself, take up his cross, and follow me. For whoever wishes to save his life will lose it, but whoever loses his life for my sake will find it. What profit would there be for one to gain the whole world and forfeit his life? Or what can one give in exchange for his life? For the Son of Man will come with his angels in his Father's glory, and then he will repay everyone according to his conduct."—Matthew 16:21-27

Once Peter and the others had made their profession of faith in Jesus as the Messiah, it was time for Jesus to make his move. He must go to Jerusalem for the final struggle. But first he will tell them precisely what's in store for them if they make this last journey with him.

"From that time on Jesus began to say plainly to his disciples, 'I must go to Jerusalem and suffer much from the elders, the chief priests, and the teachers of the Law. I will be put to death, but three days later I will be raised to life.' "

Did Jesus have miraculous knowledge of the future? Or was he simply spelling out the dangers involved in visiting Jerusalem at this time, when plots against his life were common knowledge? We don't know for sure. At any rate, he couldn't have been more explicit in pointing out the cost of discipleship. He told it like it was, and would be.

What was the effect? Well, Peter has just been designated the leader of the group, so he tries to take charge. He takes Jesus aside and gives him a friendly piece of advice. "This is no way to talk to your followers. It's bad for their morale. And we'd never let it happen, anyway. So please—no more talk of suffering and dying; it doesn't help anybody."

Peter meant well. The thought of Jesus being killed was unbearable and made no sense to him. He was a devoted, success-oriented follower, so he spoke from the heart when he urged his master to be more optimistic. So he was dumfounded when Jesus turned and lashed out at him: "Get away from me, you devil! You're in my way. You're not on the side of God, but of men!"

This is how Jesus talks to the man who, moments ago, was designated the rock on which he would build his church. One minute Peter is raised to the heights, the next he's sternly denounced as a traitor—just because he didn't want to hear of his master's suffering and death. At that moment Peter realized that he didn't know Jesus nearly as well as he had thought. People who read this passage for the first time often get the same feeling.

When we read this account today, we have the advantage of knowing why Jesus reacted so strongly to Peter's suggestion. We know that the Cross was inevitable, that Christ had to save us by his death and resurrection, so we're inclined to feel a bit superior, as though we're clued in while Peter and the others are in the dark. But are we, really? Do we understand the Cross? More important, do we *accept it?* How do you feel about suffering? Is it the one big no-no that must be avoided at all cost? If you feel that way, you have a lot of people for company, but Jesus isn't among them.

There's one more thing to note about Peter's reaction to Jesus' prediction of his fate. Did you notice what he missed? He heard Jesus speak of suffering and death, and he didn't like what he heard, and said so. But that wasn't the whole story foretold by Jesus. He also said he would rise again the third day, but by that time Peter couldn't hear, because he had stopped listening.

Did you miss it, too? It's easy to do. Suffering and death are frightening realities, and all our instincts rebel against them, so when they present themselves, we turn off our minds. And so, like Peter, we fail to hear what Jesus is trying to tell us. He was talking to *us,* as well as to the Twelve, when he told them: "If anyone wants to come with me, he must carry his cross and follow me." Terrifying words! But listen to what comes next.

"Will a person gain anything if he wins the whole world but loses his life? Of course not! There is nothing he can give to regain his life." It's a hard saying, but Jesus tells us, in no uncertain terms, that if we try to escape the Cross we'll lose everything. And then the supreme paradox: Only if we're ready to lose our lives can we hope to save them. The words would be impenetrable, if we didn't know Jesus crucified and risen from the dead. If we can believe in him and his promise, we won't find suffering and death easy to accept, but we'll be able to accept his offer of grace and its guarantee of victory.

If you feel overwhelmed by all this, don't be discouraged. The first time he said it to his followers, it went right over their heads. They just weren't ready. But the patient Christ could wait for them, as he waits for us.

THE TRANSFIGURATION

After six days Jesus took Peter, James, and John his brother, and led them up a high mountain by themselves. And he was transfigured before them; his face shone like the sun and his clothes became white as light. And behold, Moses and Elijah appeared to them, conversing with him. Then Peter said to Jesus in reply, "Lord, it is good that we are here. If you wish, I will make three tents here, one for you, one for Moses, and one for Elijah." While he was still speaking, behold, a bright cloud cast a shadow over them, then from the cloud came a voice that said, "This is my beloved Son, with whom I am well pleased; listen to him." When the disciples heard this, they fell prostrate and were very much afraid. But Jesus came and touched them, saying, "Rise, and do not be afraid." And when the disciples raised their eyes, they saw no one else but Jesus alone.

As they were coming down from the mountain, Jesus charged them, "Do not tell the vision to anyone until the Son of Man has been raised from the dead." — Matthew 17:1-9

Jesus' first prediction of his suffering and death and his attempt to put it into perspective for his followers was a failure. He had made them worried and anxious, but they were afraid to discuss the matter with him. It was like a cloud that wouldn't go away; they could only make believe it wasn't there.

But he couldn't leave it alone. The showdown was getting closer, and he had to give them something to hold onto when the going got rough. So he took the same three men — Peter, James, and John — who would later be with him during his agony in the Garden of Gethsemane. In Gethsemane they would see him at his lowest point, when fear and loathing and loneliness would render him helpless and almost crush him. But now, for a few unforgettable moments, it would be different. He took them to the lonely summit of a mountain, where in his presence they had a kind of mystical religious experience that would stay with them for the rest of their lives.

What was the meaning of those dreamlike moments when they were carried out of themselves, when time seemed to stand still and the tangible, workaday world ceased to be? Years later, Peter would write to his fellow Christians:

> We did not follow cleverly devised myths when we made known to you the power and coming of our Lord Jesus Christ, but we had been eyewitnesses of his majesty. For he received honor and glory from God the Father when that unique declaration came to him from the majestic glory, "This is my Son, my beloved, with whom I am well pleased." — 2 Peter 1:16-18

The memory of those moments on the mountain never left Peter or his companions. It was a source of strength for them, and that was what Jesus meant it to be. For a brief time, the divinity shone through, and he was no longer the down-to-earth, everyday Jesus who walked and ate and slept beside them. In a sense he always stood out from the crowd, for he was no ordinary man. But make no mistake: When God became one of us, he went all the way. He didn't just *seem* human; he was a human being in the fullest sense of the term, just like you and me. In a way, the marvel wasn't that he looked the way he did in those ecstatic moments on the mountain, but that he didn't *always* look that way. This is what St. Paul meant when he wrote to the community at Philippi about Jesus:

> Who, though he was in the form of God,
> did not regard equality with God
>   something to be grasped.
> Rather, he emptied himself,
> taking the form of a slave,
> coming in human likeness;
> and found human in appearance,

he humbled himself,
becoming obedient to death,
even death on a cross.
—Philippians 2:6-8

But for these few moments he gives his friends a glimpse of who he is, and they're carried completely out of themselves. Peter doesn't want the moment to end. Like someone trying to hold onto a beautiful dream, he begins babbling incoherently: "If you wish, I will make three tents here, one for you, one for Moses, and one for Elijah." He wants to stop the world and stay here like this forever. But even as he rambles on, the scene comes to a thunderous climax, as the cloud envelops them and the voice of God is heard: "This is my beloved Son . . . listen to him!" And they fell on their faces in fear and awe.

Later on they would recall the account of that other occasion when Moses and their fathers met God on another mountain:

On the morning of the third day there were peals of thunder and lightning, and a heavy cloud over the mountain, and a very loud trumpet blast, so that all the people in the camp trembled. But Moses led the people out of the camp to meet God, and they stationed themselves at the foot of the mountain. Mount Sinai was all wrapped in smoke, for the LORD came down upon it in fire. The smoke rose from it as though from a furnace, and the whole mountain trembled violently.

The trumpet blast grew louder and louder, while Moses was speaking and God answering him with thunder. When the LORD came down to the top of Mount Sinai, he summoned Moses to the top of the mountain, and Moses went up to him.—Exodus 19:16-20

How long they remained prostrate and trembling on the ground, they couldn't say. Was it like our dreams, that seem so long but last only seconds? At any rate, it was over as suddenly as it had begun. The next thing they knew, the cloud and the voice were gone, and Jesus was shaking them, telling them to get up. "Get up. Don't be afraid." When they looked up, everything was as before the vision. Jesus was alone, looking as he always did. And so, like men emerging from a trance, they came back to reality. Or was it the other way around?

Jesus gave his close friends a glimpse of his glory to help them through the hard times he knew were ahead for them. He still does this sometimes for us. Most of us have known peak moments when God seemed very real and close and the spiritual world felt as real as the world of sight and sound and touch. It may be at a Eucharist with our friends, when praying comes easily, when everything—music, people, gestures—seems to fit. Or it may come in moments of quiet, when we're alone without being lonely. A sunset or a flower or a deserted beach can bring on these special times when we feel in touch with ourselves and with the One who made us. Do you know what we mean?

These special moments are a blessing, but they're out of the ordinary. (That's why they're special.) Most of the time, we have to plod along without visions, without peak experiences, without even a warm feeling. That's why following Christ is different from being in a parade, and Palm Sunday was a one-shot spectacular. So was the Transfiguration on the mountain. Like the apostles when they came back to earth, we look around and see nothing out of the ordinary. Only Jesus is there, beckoning us to follow him on rainy days as well as on sunny ones. He made many promises, but one promise he never got around to making. He did not guarantee that we would never be bored.

Can you worship when you don't feel like it? Do you ever pray even when you're not in the mood? Are you kind to clods and gentle with fools? These are the times that try our souls, when sunshine patriots fall away. How about you? Are you with Christ only on mountaintops? Most of the action is in the valley.

Things to Do

1. How could the apostles be so close to Jesus and yet not grasp what he was trying to do?
2. "They had almost no appreciation of what was involved, and this was going to cost them dearly in the tragic weeks ahead." How did this work out?
3. Jesus once said, "He who is not with me is against me." Why

is it so difficult to study Jesus like any other philosopher? Why do so many people feel they have to take a stand about him, one way or another?

4. This happened to one of the authors of this book several years ago. A high school senior, taking a course on Jesus, said he could not yet give a personal answer to Christ's question, "Who do you say that I am?" And he didn't know what to do. If you were his teacher, what would you say to him?

5. Jesus' reaction to Peter's well-meant advice was so violent. Do you think he felt threatened?

6. Does an expression such as "take up your cross" have the same impact on us today as it did on the disciples of that time? Do you think today's culture makes it easier or harder for us to accept the doctrine of the Cross?

7. Why did Peter and the others ignore completely what Jesus said about the resurrection?

8. Have you ever had a peak religious moment like the Transfiguration? What brought it on, and what was it like?

9. Many people today seem to have little tolerance for boredom or routine in religious activities. In looking for "highs" and emotional satisfaction, do you think they have unrealistic expectations?

10. Is the quality of a relationship best perceived in good times or in periods of stress? Can you think of examples from your own observation or experience?

11

A Final Gift

AN EPILEPTIC BOY

When they came to the disciples, they saw a large crowd around them and scribes arguing with them. Immediately on seeing him, the whole crowd was utterly amazed. They ran up to him and greeted him. He asked them, "What are you arguing about with them?"

Someone from the crowd answered him, "Teacher, I have brought to you my son possessed by a mute spirit. Wherever it seizes him, it throws him down; he foams at the mouth, grinds his teeth, and becomes rigid. I asked your disciples to drive it out, but they were unable to do so." He said to them in reply, "O faithless generation, how long will I be with you? How long will I endure you? Bring him to me." They brought the boy to him. And when he saw him, the spirit immediately threw the boy into convulsions. As he fell to the ground, he began to roll around and foam at the mouth. Then he questioned his father, "How long has this been happening to him?" He replied, "Since childhood. It has often thrown him into fire and into water to kill him. But if you can do anything, have compassion on us and help us." Jesus said to him, " 'If you can!' Everything is possible to one who has faith."

Then the boy's father cried out, "I do believe, help my unbelief!" Jesus, on seeing a crowd rapidly gathering, rebuked the unclean spirit and said to it, "Mute and deaf spirit, I command you: come out of him and never enter him again!"

Shouting and throwing the boy into convulsions, it came out. He became like a corpse, which caused many to say, "He is dead!" But Jesus took him by the hand, raised him, and he stood up. When he entered the house, his disciples asked him in private, "Why could we not drive it out?" He said to them, "This kind can only come out through prayer."—Mark 9:14-29

When Jesus and his three companions came down from the mount of Transfiguration and rejoined the other disciples, they came upon a scene of anxiety and confusion. During their absence, a man had brought his sick boy to the disciples and asked them to cure him. They often received such requests and in the past had helped many, but this time they couldn't do anything. This left the father disappointed and their confidence shaken. There was embarrassment mixed with relief when Jesus appeared.

The father, in desperation, rushes up to get help for his son, who seems to be suffering from epilepsy. His anxiety brings a note of reproach to his voice: "I asked your disciples to drive it out, but they were unable to do so."

It doesn't happen often, but occasionally we get a glimpse of a side of Jesus that rarely appeared. He could get fed up with the people around him. His usual reaction to their pettiness, their unreasonable demands and lack of consideration was a monumental patience. But every once in a long while the exasperation would come through, and he'd tell them off. This was one of those times. As he looked around the group, he read the skepticism and the doubt in their eyes. Never mind the signs, the good works, the cures till now, they seemed to say; what have you done for us lately? So he lets them have it: "O faithless generation, how long will I be with you? How long will I endure you?"

But his annoyance wouldn't stand in the way of his compassion, so he calls for the boy, who at this moment falls into a convulsion. The boy begins to roll around and foam at the mouth.

Christ appears to ignore the boy and asks a question that sounds like someone with all the time in the world filling out a medical form. The father is beside himself. "Help us, if you possibly can!" Still Christ appears to ignore the boy rolling on the ground and begins another discussion.

The poor man has had it. In his grief and frustration, he's hit bottom. He hardly knows where he is.

"You ask me if I believe; you ask me if I trust. I don't know if I believe or not. I don't know if I trust or not. I just don't know. I can't do anything by myself anymore.

"I think I'm trying to believe. Help my unbelief! I think I'm trying to trust. Help me to trust! ... Help!"

This man was at a rock-bottom crisis. His only prayer—he doesn't even know if it is a prayer—is "Help!"

And that was enough. It was all that Jesus wanted to hear. He cures the boy and gives him back to his father.

Most of us, at one time or another, find the boy's father very easy to identify with. Consider his predicament and see if it doesn't sound familiar. He's at the end of his rope and needs help that only Jesus can give. But, as we see over and over again, Jesus can't help people unless they have faith in him. It wasn't just his enemies and his critics that he couldn't do anything for; the skeptics and the fence-sitters were disqualified, too. Without trust, nothing could happen. So what was the father to do? He couldn't just pretend to have faith; that would have been dishonest. It would have been phony to say things he didn't mean. Sure, he *wished* and *hoped* that Christ would help, but he didn't *know.* He just wasn't sure. But neither could he just walk away, for that would have meant giving up on his own son, whose health depended on a faith the father couldn't feel.

If you ever find yourself in a situation like this, it's comforting to know that Jesus accepted the father's prayer, which wasn't an act of faith but simply a request for faith. You see, anybody can *ask* for faith. Maybe you find it hard to believe (don't we all, sometimes?), but there's nothing to stop you from asking for the gift of faith. It takes just one syllable to cry "Help!"

Remember this prayer, and file it away for future reference: "Lord, I'm trying to believe. Help my unbelief!" It may come in handy some day if you ever hit rock bottom. When you hear the scraping sound, it's time for what may be the best prayer you ever said.

That feeling of hitting rock bottom, which was the experience of the boy's father and sometimes of ourselves, was soon to come to Jesus. For the last time he was on his way to Jerusalem, where betrayal and suffering and death awaited him. Time had run out; the hour of decision had struck. Jesus and his followers entered Jerusalem with the throngs of pilgrims gathered from all over the Mediterranean world for the Passover. The city was in a fever of expectation. Pontius Pilate, the Roman governor in charge of the foreign occupation forces, was taking the usual precautions against the kind of popular uprising that was always a possibility during this religious festival.

A spontaneous demonstration sprang up around the figure of Jesus, as the people waved palm branches and escorted him into the city in a kind of triumphal march. There was no violence, so the Romans took no notice; but the religious leaders watched — and didn't like what they saw. They resolved to discredit him, and for the next few days tried to trap him in religious controversy. But he turned back every attack and humiliated them in front of the people, so they decided that the only way to dispose of him and the threat he posed was to kill him.

Their chance came from an unexpected quarter. Judas came to them and offered to betray Jesus into their hands. Now the security of Jesus' inner circle could be broken. For thirty pieces of silver, they had a deal.

This was the situation on Thursday night, when Jesus and his disciples gathered to eat what they called the Passover meal, which would be known to history as the Last Supper.

THE LAST SUPPER

Before the feast of Passover, Jesus knew that his hour had come to pass from this world to the Father. He loved his own in the world and he loved them to the end. The devil had already induced Judas, son of Simon the Iscariot, to hand him over. So, during supper, fully aware that the Father had put everything into his power and that he had come from God and was returning to God, he rose from supper and took off his outer garments. He took a towel and tied it around his waist. Then he poured water into a basin and began to wash the disciples' feet and dry them with the towel around his waist. He came to Simon Peter, who said to him, "Master, are you going to wash my feet?" Jesus answered and said to him, "What I am doing, you do not understand now, but you will understand later."

Peter said to him, "You will never wash my feet."

Jesus answered him, "Unless I wash you, you will have no inheritance with me."

Simon Peter said to him, "Master, then not only my feet, but my hands and head as well."

So when he had washed their feet [and] put his garments back on and reclined at table again, he said to them, "Do you realize what I have done for you? You call me 'teacher' and 'master,' and rightly so, for indeed I am. If I, therefore, the master and teacher, have washed your feet, you ought to wash one another's feet. I have given you a model to follow, so that as I have done for you, you should also do.

"I give you a new commandment: love one another. As I have loved you, so you also should love one another. This is how all will know that you are my disciples, if you have love for one another." — John 13:1-9, 12-15, 34-35

The fateful hour had arrived. Jesus had a few hours of freedom left, a few more hours of life. His disciples weren't ready for this final struggle; all his efforts to prepare them had failed. Now he would take his last meal with them, his Last Supper. Every word, every gesture was charged with special meaning which only he could grasp now; they would come to understand much later.

The first gesture, which surprised and troubled them, was the washing of the feet. It was customary at that time that when a guest came to the house, a servant would wash the dust from his feet. The servant, who was the low man on the totem pole, must have been the one who got stuck with this job.

The disciples are amazed when Jesus takes on this lowly task, and good old impetuous Peter manages to put his foot in it again.

"No, sir," says Peter, "you're not going to wash *my* feet."

"Look," says Christ, "this is very important. Don't get stubborn."

Peter says, "Lord, I'm a dummy. Wash my feet—and you better wash this thick head of mine, while you're at it."

After washing the disciples' feet, Christ returns to the table. "Do you understand what this is all about? I've given you a sign of love. I've given you an example of love. I've been giving you love for the last couple of years. I want you to love one another the way I love you."

One of the pairs of feet belonged to Judas, the man who had sold him out to his enemies. What went through the minds of Jesus and Judas at that moment? Was Jesus making one last attempt to move that stony heart? Did Judas feel a twinge of shame at receiving this mark of deference from the master he had betrayed? We'll never know. But one thing we do know: The love that Jesus Christ has for sinners is something very special. Most of us, no matter how easygoing or thick-skinned we are, put limits on how forgiving we will be. That's just one of the differences between us and the Savior of the world. It's even harder to forgive those who've been close to us. For a couple of years, Judas lived very close to Jesus. They traveled, ate, and slept in each other's company. They had shared secrets, confided in each other, gone through good times and bad together. And now it has come to this: Judas is a traitor, and the man he betrayed is washing his feet.

There are two messages here for us—an encouragement and a warning. No matter what I've done, no matter how badly I've messed up, Christ believes in me and sees possibilities when everyone else (including myself) has given up on me. No matter how badly or how often I've let him down, he reaches out to me in forgiveness and love. If he can wash the feet of Judas, he can put up with me.

But this doesn't mean I can take him for granted. If I resist his grace and persist in my selfishness or dishonesty or cruelty, I run the risk of pushing myself over the line, past the point of no return, where he can no longer reach me. That's what happened to Judas, who was once very close to Christ, one of his inner circle of intimate friends. And if it could happen to him, it could happen to anyone, including me. Not that Jesus gives up on anyone; he never does. But any relationship can die when one of the parties hardens his or her heart and makes reconciliation impossible. If the tragedy of Judas tells us anything, it tells us that even the limitless love of Christ can be turned off forever by the human heart.

> Then he took the bread, said the blessing, broke it, and gave it to them, saying, "This is my body, which will be given for you; do this in memory of me." And likewise the cup after they had eaten, saying, "This cup is the new covenant in my blood, which will be shed for you." — Luke 22:19, 20

Then a marvelous thing happened. Christ took bread, gave it to those who were with him, and said, "This is my body." After eating, he did the same with the cup, saying, "This cup is the new covenant in my blood, which will be shed for you." He told those with him to do this in the future as a remembrance of him.

To a certain extent, the apostles understood at that time what was happening. But it was only later, under the influence of the Holy Spirit, that they began to grasp its full significance. In fact, throughout their lives they had a deeper and deeper experience of it.

Why did Jesus give us the Eucharist? Because he wants to be with us. When you love someone very much, you want to be with that person and share your life with him or her. When God became human in Jesus Christ and died for us, it seemed that he could do no more to show his love. But he went even further. He found a way to be with us always, to be our very food under the form of bread and wine. That's what *comm-union* means — being joined in a union too intimate and astounding for our minds to grasp.

If just once in the history of the world the Son of God gave himself to human beings this way, it would be a wonderful thing. But this isn't something that took place just once, at a certain time in a certain place. It happens today, every day, whenever

Christians meet to celebrate the Eucharist. When priest and people join in the Mass, Christ becomes truly present on the altar and gives himself to us as he gave himself to the apostles on the first Holy Thursday. In Holy Communion he is as close to us as he was to his little band of followers in the supper room that fateful night.

Catholics often complain and argue about the Mass. They complain about the homilies and the music. They argue about whether they should have to attend every Sunday. "Why can't I stay home and talk to God?" is a question often asked. Some young people say it's a bore. "It's like an old rerun on TV," said one student.

These are real problems that are important to many people, and we cannot just dismiss them. How do we answer them? Well, start at the beginning. The Eucharist was never intended to be entertaining or to compete with television or concerts. It's a sacred action at the heart of our religion, in which Christ gives himself to us, his people. If that isn't important to me, then the most eloquent homilies, the best music, and the friendliest gatherings of the nicest people won't turn me on.

Sure, the priest should try to preach well. The choir should practice. The planning and participation in the liturgy are important. But even when these are uninspired—and it's hard to be inspiring every week—we must remember the heart of the matter. Jesus Christ, the Son of God, is right here in our midst, and he wants to be united with me and with those around me. To some people the friendship of Christ is so important that they find it hard to be bored at the Eucharist, and if the boredom happens, they can put up with it. That's the way it is with the most important relationships in our lives: They can survive boredom and rise above dullness and routine.

Things to Do

1. The health of the epileptic boy ultimately depended on his father's ability to make some kind of act of faith in Jesus. Does this seem right? What does it tell us about the way God deals with people?
2. Have you ever been in a predicament like the father's? How

did you handle it? What would you do next time?
3. Do you think it was hard for Jesus to wash Judas's feet?
4. How could Judas be so close to Jesus for so long and end up the way he did?
5. Can the Eucharist mean anything to a person who doesn't have a personal relationship with Jesus?
6. If we had this relationship, would most of our problems with the Mass be solved?
7. Have you ever had a relationship that survived boredom and routine?

12

Tragedy

THE AGONY IN THE GARDEN

Then Jesus came with them to a place called Gethsemane, and he said to his disciples, "Sit here while I go over there and pray." He took along Peter and the two sons of Zebedee, and began to feel sorrow and distress. Then he said to them, "My soul is sorrowful even to death. Remain here and keep watch with me." He advanced a little and fell prostrate in prayer, saying, "My Father, if it is possible, let this cup pass from me; yet, not as I will, but as you will." When he returned to his disciples he found them asleep. He said to Peter, "So you could not keep watch with me for one hour? Watch and pray that you may not undergo the test. The spirit is willing, but the flesh is weak." Withdrawing a second time, he prayed again, "My Father, if it is not possible that this cup pass without my drinking it, your will be done!" Then he returned once more and found them asleep, for they could not keep their eyes open. He left them and withdrew again and prayed a third time, saying the same thing again. Then he returned to his disciples and said to them, "Are you still sleeping and taking your rest? Behold, the hour is at hand when the Son of Man is to be handed over to sinners. Get up, let us go. Look, my betrayer is at hand."

While he was still speaking, Judas, one of the Twelve, arrived, accompanied by a large crowd, with swords and clubs, who had come from the chief priests and the elders of the people. His betrayer had arranged a sign with them, saying, "The man I shall kiss is the one; arrest him." Immediately he went over to Jesus and said, "Hail, Rabbi!" and he kissed him. Jesus answered him, "Friend, do what you have come for." Then stepping forward they laid hands on Jesus and arrested him. And behold, one of those who accompanied Jesus put his hand to his sword, drew it, and struck the high priest's servant, cutting off his ear. Then Jesus said to him, "Put your sword back into its sheath, for all who take the sword will perish by the sword. Do you think that I cannot call upon my Father and he will not provide me at this moment with more than twelve legions of angels? But then how would the scriptures be fulfilled which say that it must come to pass this way?" At that hour Jesus said to the crowds, "Have you come out as against a robber, with swords and clubs to seize me? Day after day I sat teaching in the temple area, yet you did not arrest me. But all this has come to pass that the writings of the prophets may be fulfilled." Then all the disciples left him and fled. — Matthew 26:36-56

The only one of the Twelve who was alert that night was Judas, and he was bent on Jesus' destruction. It was too bad, for if ever Jesus needed friends, it was during those last few hours before his arrest.

After the supper, they went to a garden outside the city. Judas, of course, had left during the supper to make arrangements for Christ's arrest. The garden would be an ideal place for the ambush: He had often gone there before, and they could seize him without the populace being aware of it. The authorities were afraid to make an arrest in public; his followers might provoke a riot.

Jesus and his friends were quiet as they entered the garden. He was silent and withdrawn, and they felt a sense of foreboding. The dinner, the wine, and their nameless fears made them tired and sleepy. They wouldn't be of much help to him tonight.

As the crisis drew near, Jesus experienced an overpowering feeling of sorrow, fear, and loneliness. He realized that terrible things were about to happen to him, and he wanted out. He felt the onrush of terror and dread, and he wanted to run away from the whole thing.

There have always been people who believed that Jesus was the Son of God but who could not quite convince themselves that he was truly human, like you and me. Without putting it into words, they have thought of him as God playing a part, making believe he was human. But that's not the way it was. He experienced to the full all the frailties (except sin) that are part of the human condition. His sorrow, his fear, his loneliness were all too real. They almost defeated him.

In this crisis, as he has done before, he tries to pray. But his Father seems remote, aloof, far away. In desperation he asks to be spared the ordeal that's rushing upon him, but even as the words escape his lips, he rejects them. A titanic struggle is being waged within his soul. "My Father, if it is possible, take this cup of suffering from me! Yet not what I want, but what you want." He knows in his heart of hearts that his ordeal will end in triumph, and that it is of tremendous importance to others.

He brings his burden not only to God but also to his friends, so they can share it with him. Although he goes off by himself, he leads Peter, James, and John to a spot close by. These are the three who saw his glory on the mount of Transfiguration. Now they will see him at his lowest point, beaten and crushed by the terror that drains the very blood from his pores. He wants them to hear his prayer, to know how he feels, to share his loneliness and fear. He's saying, "Look, I can't take this thing by myself. Please help me. I need you."

At this desperate moment he prays and then comes over to find them asleep. He wakes them up and asks them to share his prayer. Guilt and shame make them promise to stand by him, but weariness lulls them to sleep again, leaving him terribly alone. If he had asked them to draw swords and fight, they would probably have sprung to his aid. But this time he didn't want them to *do* anything; he just wanted them to *be* there with him in his hour of need, and they failed him. The one time that God needed us humans, we let God down.

We all have had the experience, too many times, of being let down by people. Friends are rarely as dependable as we want

them to be. Sometimes we cope with this by trying to cut ourselves off from all dependence on others, by pursuing the unat-
tainable goal of self-sufficiency. Or, by amassing wealth and
power over others, we try to guarantee that help will never be
lacking, because we've bought it with money or influence. These
are ways we try to escape from the human condition, which
decrees that people will always need people, no matter how
shaky or unsatisfactory the arrangement. When God became
one of us in Jesus Christ, he went all the way, even to depending
on weak, sinful people who deserted him in his hour of greatest
need. This is how he tells us that if we want to become real
people, we must count on others, even at the risk of betrayal.

Speaking of betrayals, here comes Judas with his motley band
of Temple guards and security police. Judas and Jesus meet for
the last time in the murky groves of Gethsemane, whose shadows
mirror the darkness in the traitor's heart. Christ is face-to-face
with his most spectacular failure. It may seem strange to say it,
but you could make out a good case for describing Jesus as an
underachiever. After all, his main work was with people, and
here, a few hours before his death, what has he accomplished?
A trusted friend betrays him, and his inner circle of followers
runs from the garden in panic. Tomorrow the crowd, which has
never understood him, will cry for his blood, and his enemies'
triumph will be complete. It's no exaggeration to say that few
people have had as little to show for their lives at the moment
of death as did Jesus of Nazareth. The ultimate humiliation, the
kiss of Judas, said it all.

THE JUDGMENT OF PILATE

When it was morning, all the chief priests and the elders
of the people took counsel against Jesus to put him to
death. They bound him, led him away, and handed him
over to Pilate, the governor [—Matthew 27:1-2]. They
brought charges against him, saying, "We found this man
misleading our people; he opposes the payment of taxes
to Caesar and maintains that he is the Messiah, a king."
—Luke 23:2

So Pilate went back into the praetorium and summoned

Jesus and said to him, "Are you the King of the Jews?" Jesus answered, "Do you say this on your own or have others told you about me?"

Pilate answered, "I am not a Jew, am I? Your own nation and the chief priests handed you over to me. What have you done?"

Jesus answered, "My kingdom does not belong to this world. If my kingdom did belong to this world, my attendants [would] be fighting to keep me from being handed over to the Jews. But as it is, my kingdom is not here."

So Pilate said to him, "Then you are a king?"

Jesus answered, "You say I am a king. For this I was born and for this I came into the world, to testify to the truth. Everyone who belongs to the truth listens to my voice."

Pilate said to him, "What is truth?" —John 18:33-38

Pilate then summoned the chief priests, the rulers, and the people and said to them, "You brought this man to me and accused him of inciting the people to revolt. I have conducted my investigation in your presence and have not found this man guilty of the charges you have brought against him, nor did Herod, for he sent him back to us. So no capital crime has been committed by him. Therefore I shall have him flogged and then release him." —Luke 23:13-16

Then Pilate took Jesus and had him scourged. And the soldiers wove a crown out of thorns and placed it on his head, and clothed him in a purple cloak, and they came to him and said, "Hail, King of the Jews!" And they struck him repeatedly.

Once more Pilate went out and said to them, "Look, I am bringing him out to you, so that you may know that I find no guilt in him." So Jesus came out, wearing the crown of thorns and the purple cloak. And he said to them, "Behold, the man!"

When the chief priests and the guards saw him they cried out, "Crucify him, crucify him!"

Pilate said to them, "Take him yourselves and crucify him. I find no guilt in him."

The Jews answered, "We have a law, and according to that law he ought to die, because he made himself the Son of God."

Now when Pilate heard this statement, he became even more afraid, and went back into the praetorium and said to Jesus, "Where are you from?" Jesus did not answer him. So Pilate said to him, "Do you not speak to me? Do you not know that I have power to release you and I have power to crucify you?"

Jesus answered [him], "You would have no power over me if it had not been given to you from above. For this reason the one who handed me over to you has the greater sin."

Consequently, Pilate tried to release him; but the Jews cried out, "If you release him, you are not a friend of Caesar. Everyone who makes himself a king opposes Caesar." —John 19:1-12

When Pilate saw that he was not succeeding at all, but that a riot was breaking out instead, he took water and washed his hands in the sight of the crowd, saying, "I am innocent of this man's blood. Look to it yourselves" [—Matthew 27:24]. Then he handed him over to them to be crucified. —John 19:16

In the final scene of the movie *Judgment at Nuremberg,* Spencer Tracy confronts Burt Lancaster in the latter's prison cell. Tracy, an American jurist, has sentenced Lancaster, a convicted Nazi war criminal. As a civil judge, Lancaster had bowed to pressure from Hitler and had knowingly condemned innocent defendants, who were then sent to the concentration camps. In the film, Lancaster acknowledges his guilt and the justice of his sentence, but in a final private meeting he pleads with Tracy not to judge him too harshly in his mind. "I want you to know . . . you must understand . . . I never thought it would come to this [the concentration camps]." Tracy looks long and hard at him, and the movie audience expects a word of pardon, or at least of understanding, a recognition that he did not foresee the horror of the camps. Instead, he says, "It came to this the first time you condemned an innocent man."

The cell door clangs shut, Tracy leaves, and the film ends.

Pontius Pilate never thought it would come to crucifixion. True, the case of the Priests vs. Jesus would not have come before him if the plaintiffs were not seeking the death penalty. Under the terms of the occupation of Judea, the death sentence was reserved to the Roman governor. But he was confident he could settle the case without taking any extreme measures. Throughout the hours of that Friday morning, he twisted and turned and tried every gambit he knew, to save the life of this apparently harmless man. But he lost the fight, and Jesus forfeited his life, almost at the very start of the proceedings.

After hearing the charges of sedition, Pilate examines the defendant, is convinced of his innocence, and so informs his accusers: "I have not found this man guilty." And that should have been the end of it, right there. His next words should have been, "Therefore I will let him go." Instead, he makes a fatal error. He tries to compromise, to come up with something for everybody. The governor had the power to ram an acquittal down their throats, but politics and public relations made it advisable for him to get along with the Temple authorities and avoid friction as much as possible. That was Roman policy in occupied territories. If he just did the right thing and let Jesus go free, the religious leaders would lose face. So, to sweeten the pill of an adverse judgment, he decrees: "I shall have him flogged and release him."

Punish him for what? For being innocent? For being falsely accused? For getting caught in the middle of a power struggle between corrupt and powerful men? Pilate thought he could have it both ways. He forgot that justice and compromise almost never go together.

It is fascinating and disturbing to trace the steps of that morning's encounter between Jesus and Pilate. At first the governor is haughty and detached, intent on dispensing impersonal justice. But as the drama progresses, he is struck by the quiet dignity and strength of the prisoner. It unsettles him, makes him less sure of himself. "You will not speak to me? Remember, I have the authority to set you free and also to have you crucified." During the course of the interrogations there is a subtle reversal of roles, so that Jesus sounds like the judge and Pilate like the accused: "You have authority only because it was given to you by God. So the man who handed me over to you is guilty of a worse sin."

The governor, thrown off balance by this disquieting man, realizes at one point that he is in danger of being personally touched by him. We have witnessed this phenomenon before. Remember Zacchaeus? The Samaritan woman? Like them, Pilate came under Jesus' spell and almost found his inner, rock-bottom self. Just in time, he stepped back and put on one of the masks we all save for those occasions when we want to avoid seeing ourselves for what we really are. This was the mask of the sophisticated skeptic, the cultivated Roman who spurned religion as superstition. "Do you think I am a Jew? . . . And what is truth?"

Still he tries to avoid a total sellout. He wants the impossible: to be fair, but not *too* fair. He wants to dispense justice, but not *too* much. He wants to tell the truth, but not at the expense of important people's feelings. He wants to respect religion, but not get involved in it. Why can't the priests be more reasonable? Why won't Jesus bend a little and help him? Damn these single-minded, fanatical Jews! No wonder they're down and Rome is up! They don't know the First Rule for Getting Ahead! "To get along, you go along."

He's holding out, playing for time, but the priests know he's hooked, and all they have to do is reel him in. At last they play their trump card: "If you release this man, you are no friend of Caesar."

That does it. When the chips are down, you have to stick up for what's important. If he doesn't commit judicial murder and execute Jesus, these vengeful men will see to it that Caesar, back in Rome, gets a bad report on him. Think what that would mean. No more governor's palace, with free limousine service and padded expense account. No more swimming pool. Goodbye stereo system and dancing girls. Okay, guys, you win. Take him away. Just give me some water, so I can wash his blood off my hands. Don't blame me: It's his own fault. A man has to protect his own. I mean, survival is what it's all about, right? I didn't want to hurt anybody, just do right by my family. A lot of people depend on me, and I owe them something. But I never thought it would come to this.

So they took Jesus away, scourged him, and crowned him with thorns, dragged him outside the city, and crucified him.

From Gethsemane to Calvary, the physical sufferings he undergoes are so barbaric that we shrink in horror from contemplating them. But the torments he endures are not only of the body but also of the mind, the spirit, the feelings, the emotions.

He experiences distress and fear and the overpowering desire to run away from it all. Betrayed and abandoned by his friends, he knows what it is to be alone. Promises made to him are broken. He is falsely accused, interrogated, and judged by hypocrites. He is blindfolded, made the butt of jokes, and brutally struck. They drag him through the streets, dress him up like a king, and treat him like a fool.

As he hangs on the cross in excruciating pain, he is despised, gloated over, and mocked. Nearly all his friends have run away. A tremendous sense of loneliness and depression comes over him, the feeling of being totally alone and utterly helpless. He feels that even his Father has abandoned him. In this extremity of bodily and mental anguish, he cries out, "My God, my God, why did you abandon me?" He receives no answer, no relief, and dies alone.

Think of the evil in your own life. Consider not only your personal sins but also all the sorrows, difficulties, and disorientations that afflict your body and mind. Omit nothing that is confusing, lonely, and painful. Include even the transition from the phase of your life to the next phase—the transition called death. And realize that *you no longer suffer these alone.* Christ has taken on everything in your life that brings you guilt, pain, confusion, loneliness, and fear. From now on, you two share it together.

The theologian can identify the evil in your life in a minute but can't explain it in a lifetime.

The theologian can tell you that God can draw good from the evil in your life. This is fine as you sit there comfortably and listen. This is not fine when you begin to hurt.

When you hurt, theoretical explanations don't offer much comfort.

When you hurt—whether in your body or in your feelings, in the midst of utter boredom or of such spiritual confusion that you don't even know if you believe or trust in God—perhaps all you can do at a time like that is cry "Help!" and ask Christ on the cross to take you by the hand.

Things to Do

1. Have you ever had to cope with fear in order to do something important? How did you handle it? Do you ever pray in such a situation? Has your prayer ever been answered?
2. Have you ever been let down by people you depended on? Did you ever disappoint someone who needed your help?
3. Is it accurate to describe Jesus as a failure?
4. What was the weakness in Pilate that assured Jesus' conviction?
5. Does this sort of thing go on today? Where? Are the same causes at work?
6. Would Pilate have been better off if he had never met Jesus? How can Jesus be bad for people?

13

Triumph

THE RISEN CHRIST

On the evening of that first day of the week, when the doors were locked, where the disciples were, for fear of the Jews, Jesus came and stood in their midst and said to them, "Peace be with you." — John 20:19

But they were startled and terrified and thought that they were seeing a ghost. Then he said to them, "Why are you troubled? And why do questions arise in your hearts? Look at my hands and my feet, that it is I myself. Touch me and see, because a ghost does not have flesh and bones as you can see I have." And as he said this, he showed them his hands and his feet.

While they were still incredulous for joy and were amazed, he asked them, "Have you anything here to eat?" They gave him a piece of baked fish; he took it and ate it in front of them.

He said to them, "These are my words that I spoke to you while I was still with you, that everything written about me in the law of Moses and in the prophets and psalms must be fulfilled." Then he opened their minds to understand the scriptures. — Luke 24:37-45

[Jesus] said to them again, "Peace be with you. As the Father has sent me, so I send you." And when he had said this, he breathed on them and said to them, "Receive the holy Spirit. Whose sins you forgive are forgiven them, and whose sins you retain are retained."

Thomas, called Didymus, one of the Twelve, was not with them when Jesus came. So the other disciples said to him, "We have seen the Lord." But he said to them, "Unless I see the mark of the nails in his hands and put my finger into the nailmarks and put my hand into his side, I will not believe."

Now a week later his disciples were again inside and Thomas was with them. Jesus came, although the doors were locked, and stood in their midst and said, "Peace be with you." Then he said to Thomas, "Put your finger here and see my hands, and bring your hand and put it into my side, and do not be unbelieving, but believe."

Thomas answered and said to him, "My Lord and my God!"

Jesus said to him, "Have you come to believe because you have seen me? Blessed are those who have not seen and have believed." — John 20:21-29

An old saying has it that it's never so dark as just before the dawn. This was certainly true for Jesus' followers on the first Easter Sunday.

The past week they'd had enough shocks to last them a lifetime. A week ago they had accompanied him on a triumphal march into Jerusalem to celebrate the feast of national liberation, the Passover. The waving palm branches and the enthusiastic shouts of the crowd created in them the illusion that they were in the front ranks of a popular movement destined to sweep all before it. They thought a revolution was in the offing and that they'd be the key people in the New Order, with Jesus at their head. How long ago that seemed now! The arrest of their leader on Thursday, his trial before Pilate on Friday, and his swift and horrible execution seemed like a nightmare from which they couldn't awaken. All their hopes and ambitions lay in ruins, and they'd lost even the will to put the shattered pieces of their lives together again.

The scene we've quoted takes place in the evening. The disciples are huddled together in fear and grief. The authorities have done away with Jesus, and it might well be his friends' turn next. Terror has locked and bolted the doors of the supper room, but despair has locked their minds and hearts. Disillusionment has robbed them of their dreams. They're without hope, wallowing in self-pity, tortured by remorse, paralyzed by fear.

And it's at this moment of impenetrable gloom that the Light bursts upon them. Even though the doors are shut, Jesus comes and stands before them. "Shalom," he says. "Peace."

The disciples panic. They've seen him dead and buried, so this must be a ghost. After all that's happened this is just too much, and they're beside themselves with fright.

But he talks to them, gently, calmly, quieting their fear. "What are you afraid of? This isn't a disembodied spirit. It's really me. Look, I'm eating this fish; ghosts don't eat. Here, touch me. Don't be afraid." Gradually their fright and disbelief subside, and the peace he has wished them fills their hearts with a joy such as they've never known or dreamed of. Calm mingles with their exhilaration, and he explains to them that he had to suffer and die, that he has risen from the dead, that his triumph is complete. They're together once more, and nothing can ever separate them again.

Remember, these are the same disciples who had abandoned him just a few days before. These are the friends who had sworn at the Last Supper that they'd stand by him, and then had run away.

"Peace," Christ says again. And this "Peace" is more than a greeting. It has a fullness of meaning, and part of that meaning is forgiveness of their failure.

Christ then gives them the awesome power to forgive sins. It's the right moment to confer this gift. Forgiveness is for *sinners,* and so it's to sinners that he gives the power to forgive. In effect, he's saying to them: "When others come to you with their sins and their faults, remember that you, too, have fallen on your face. Keep that in mind, and help them out, as I have helped you."

It's a medically proven fact that some bones, after being broken and set, mend and become stronger than before. Relationships are subject to the same paradox. You'd think that friends who never disagreed would be closer than those who have broken up and come together again, but it isn't necessarily so. Lovers are rarely so close as when they've just kissed and made up after a quarrel. It was that way between Jesus and his followers, and it's that way between God and us. There's something special between the shepherd and the lost sheep, and it wouldn't be there if the sheep had never strayed from the flock. We're not saying that people should stray or sin. We're just paraphrasing Jesus himself, who said that there would be more joy in heaven over one repentant sinner than over ninety-nine who had nothing to repent. Don't try to figure it out. The heart has reasons that the mind can never understand.

Thomas wasn't there for all of this. How fortunate for us! Whatever kept him away that first Easter Sunday evening, it was a good break for those of us who need a little extra help from our friends to believe the Good News.

Why didn't Thomas believe the others when they told him they had seen the Lord? Well, he had been burned once already. He had staked everything on Jesus and seen his hopes go down the drain on Good Friday. That kind of disillusionment he didn't need again. Thomas fell into the classic trap that most of us fall into at one time or another: He tried to insulate himself against disappointment by swearing off faith and trust. Fortunately, he didn't keep his pledge, or he would have shriveled up as a human being.

Jesus went an extra mile to save Thomas from his self-defeating, corrosive doubt. And in doing so, he spoke an encouraging word for all of us who, like Thomas, find it hard to believe and would rather see for ourselves.

"Do you believe because you see me? How happy are those who believe without seeing me!"

We're tempted to envy the disciples, to wish that we could meet the risen Christ face-to-face as they did. We see that encounter as something very special. But Jesus tells us that *we* are the ones who are special, for we believe without seeing and thus accept from his hand the gift of faith. Nothing turned Jesus on more than people's faith in him. In this he was like most of us. And he hasn't changed a bit.

THE ROAD TO EMMAUS

Now that very day two of them were going to a village seven miles from Jerusalem called Emmaus, and they were conversing about all the things that had occurred. And it happened that while they were conversing and debating, Jesus himself drew near and walked with them, but their eyes were prevented from recognizing him. He asked them, "What are you discussing as you walk along?" They stopped, looking downcast. One of them, named Cleopas, said to him in reply, "Are you the only visitor to Jerusalem who does not know of the things that have taken place there in these days?" And he replied to them, "What sort of things?" They said to him, "The things that happened to Jesus the Nazarene, who was a prophet mighty in deed and word before God and all the people, how our chief priests and rulers both handed him over to a sentence of death and crucified him. But we were hoping that he would be the one to redeem Israel; and besides all this, it is now the third day since this took place. Some women from our group, however, have astounded us: they were at the tomb early in the morning and did not find his body; they came back and reported that they had indeed seen a vision of angels who announced that he was alive.

"Then some of those with us went to the tomb and found things just as the women had described, but him they did not see." And he said to them, "Oh, how foolish you are! How slow of heart to believe all that the prophets spoke! Was it not necessary that the Messiah should suffer these things and enter into his glory?" Then beginning with Moses and all the prophets, he interpreted to them what referred to him in all the scriptures. As they approached the village to which they were going, he gave the impression that he was going on farther. But they urged him, "Stay with us, for it is nearly evening and the day is almost over." So he went in to stay with them. And it happened that, while he was with them at table, he took bread, said the blessing, broke it, and gave it to them. With that their eyes were opened and they recognized him, but he vanished from their sight. Then they said to each other, "Were not our hearts burning [within us] while he spoke to us on the way and opened the scriptures to us?" So they set out at once and returned to Jerusalem where they found gathered together the eleven and those with them who were saying, "The Lord has truly been raised and has appeared to Simon!"

Then the two recounted what had taken place on the way and how he was made known to them in the breaking of the bread. — Luke 24:13-35

It was on the afternoon of that first Easter Sunday that Cleopas and his friend met the risen Jesus. There are many mysterious things about this meeting, but the first is that they didn't recognize him. There are several other instances in the Gospel accounts of the post-Resurrection Jesus in which the same thing happens: People who had been close to him in life do not know him at first, but then perceive his identity in a flash of recognition.

In all these scenes, one thing must be kept in mind. The disciples are experiencing a reality which no words, no language, can fully express. We're dealing here with a mystery — the mystery of Christ's resurrected body.

As usual, there are two sides to the mystery: His resurrected body is *real,* and it is *changed.* Or put it another way: It's really Jesus, but he's different. His body is radically transformed, but not destroyed. He can eat, but he needs no food. He can be touched, yet he is free of the bounds of time and space. Radiant in triumph, he is forever more a stranger to weariness and pain and loneliness. He who drank the cup of suffering to the dregs and laid down his life has banished sorrow and defeated death.

But he looked like just another friendly stranger that Sunday afternoon when he joined the two grieving disciples on the way to Emmaus. He shows an interest in them and expresses concern at their sadness and dejection. To his gentle prodding, they respond by unburdening themselves of their sorrow. They tell him of the terrible things that have happened, the great things that might have been, the beautiful things that now can never be. It's a story of dashed expectations and of dreams laid waste. "We had hoped . . . " But we hope no longer. It's finished, and so are we.

Up to this point, Jesus has just been a good listener. When people are down, the way Cleopas and his friend were, the best thing we can give them is a willing ear. If I'm scraping the bottom and you're my friend, I don't want words from you. Just be with me and care.

Jesus did that and more. He speaks words not of empty comfort, but of brilliant insight. Recalling the history of their people, the story of God's ways with men, he helps the travelers to see that a suffering Messiah meant not the end of their hopes, but the fulfillment of God's saving plan.

As they come under his spell, their burden somehow becomes lighter, and they begin to feel at peace with themselves. Before they know it, they've arrived at their destination.

Then the stranger says good-bye and makes as though to continue his journey. But they're concerned: It's getting dark, the roads are unsafe, he's been on foot a long time. So they offer him their hospitality. "Stay with us." Such a small gesture of thoughtfulness—and such a great reward! In "the breaking of the bread"—a phrase that sounds very much like the Eucharist—they experience the unforgettable moment of recognition: It's he. And just as quickly it's over, and he's gone.

"Were not our hearts burning within us while he spoke to us on the way and opened the scriptures to us?" Yes, and they know the flame will never die. He has vanished from their sight, but no matter; he lives. He's with them, and nothing can ever take him away. So this is how we meet the risen Christ, you and I—through a kind word, by an unselfish invitation, in the Breaking of the Bread. He comes unexpectedly, is not always recognized, is glad to be asked, but forces himself on no one. To see him, I must be as alert to the needs of others as to my own. He waits for me in the guise of a needy stranger or a suffering friend and under the appearances of bread and wine. Only the eyes of faith can pierce the veil, but one moment of vision is worth a lifetime.

Finally, to recognize the risen Jesus is to catch a glimpse of the person I'm destined to be. When Christ conquered death, he did it for us all. The gift of eternal life is offered to those who will take it. What will that life be like? We don't know. " 'What eye has not seen, and ear has not heard, and what has not entered the human heart, what God has prepared for those who love him,' this God has revealed to us through the Spirit" (1 Corinthians 2:9).

But we're given a sign: the resurrected body of Jesus. Like him, we will suffer and die, but we will not be destroyed. We will be changed, remarkably changed for the better:

> Behold, God's dwelling is with the human race. He will dwell with them and they will be his people and God himself will always be with them [as their God]. He will wipe every tear from their eyes, and there shall be no more death or mourning, wailing or pain, [for] the old order has passed away.—Revelation 21:3, 4

And all our heart wishes will be fulfilled, beyond our wildest dreams. When Christ triumphed in his resurrection, he defeated everything (including death) that is painful, confusing, difficult, lonely. By his total victory over sin and death, he gained everything (including resurrection) that the heart can wish for.

"Okay, so Jesus triumphed. (Nice going, Jesus!) But what does that have to do with me?"

Everything. His resurrection is the source of every triumph in your life. Because he rose, you can now attain everything (including resurrection) that your heart can wish for.

By yourself, you can never gain these things. Together with the risen Christ, you can. From now on, you two strive together to attain your heart wishes. You are no longer alone.

TONGUES OF FIRE

When the time for Pentecost was fulfilled, they were all in one place together. And suddenly there came from the sky a noise like a strong driving wind, and it filled the entire house in which they were. Then there appeared to them tongues as of fire, which parted and came to rest on each one of them. And they were all filled with the holy Spirit and began to speak in different tongues, as the Spirit enabled them to proclaim.

Now there were devout Jews from every nation under heaven staying in Jerusalem. At this sound, they gathered in a large crowd, but they were confused because each one heard them speaking in his own language. They were astounded, and in amazement they asked, "Are not all these people who are speaking Galileans? Then how does each of us hear them in his own native language?" — Acts 2:1-8

They were all astounded and bewildered, and said to one another, "What does this mean?" But others said, scoffing, "They have had too much new wine."

Then Peter stood up with the Eleven, raised his voice, and proclaimed to them, "You who are Jews, indeed all of you staying in Jerusalem. Let this be known to you, and listen to my words. These people are not drunk, as you suppose, for it is only nine o'clock in the morning." — Acts 2:12-15

"You who are Israelites, hear these words. Jesus the Nazorean was a man commended to you by God with mighty deeds, wonders, and signs, which God worked through him in your midst, as you yourselves know. This man, delivered up by the set plan and foreknowledge of God, you killed, using lawless men to crucify him." — Acts 2:22-23

"Exalted at the right hand of God, he received the promise of the holy Spirit from the Father and poured it forth, as you see and hear." — Acts 2:33

"Therefore let the whole house of Israel know for certain that God has made him both Lord and Messiah, this Jesus whom you crucified."

Now when they heard this, they were cut to the heart, and they asked Peter and the other apostles, "What are we to do, my brothers?" Peter [said] to them, "Repent and be baptized, every one of you, in the name of Jesus Christ for the forgiveness of your sins; and you will receive the gift of the holy Spirit. For the promise is made to you and to your children and to all those far off, whomever the Lord our God will call."

He testified with many other arguments, and was exhorting them, "Save yourselves from this corrupt generation." Those who accepted his message were baptized,

and about three thousand persons were added that day.
—Acts 2:36-41

The risen Jesus didn't stay long with his followers—just long enough to confirm their faith in him and in themselves for the great work that was about to begin. He had told them he must go, so that he might send the Holy Spirit to confirm them in their mission of carrying the Good News to the ends of the earth.

When the Spirit came upon them, the results were spectacular. People were deeply moved. An extraordinary change came over them, and they began to understand, much more deeply, all that Christ said and did. Where at an earlier date all was confusion and "in one ear and out the other," now there is a profound experience of the meaning. They themselves have come alive as people. There's a courage and a strength that was missing before. There's a peace that isn't their own. There's a capacity to grow. There's a meeting with God, and in the Holy Spirit there's a meeting with others. From now on, they belong to God and to one another.

And there's a desire to share all this with other people.

Notice the symbol of fire—a very apt symbol indeed. With one match I can start a bonfire. Fire spreads, and so will this community of Christ's friends called church. So will this influence of the Holy Spirit. Prompted by the Spirit, Christ's friends want to share him with others.

Of course, no matter how marvelously God works among people, God doesn't overpower them and force them to believe. The response of faith is free. Even on this great day, there were a few wise guys who weren't impressed. These cynics kept their skepticism intact and successfully resisted any danger of religious experience by making fun of the whole scene: "These people are all smashed; they're nuts." Peter has an easy answer for that one: It's only nine o'clock in the morning, much too early for all these people to be drunk.

Then Peter gets serious and is inspired to make the best speech of his life. This man who, a couple of months ago, caved in before the taunts of a servant girl and denied Christ, now stands before his people and calls them to repent and be converted. He tells them of God's plan, of Christ, of the gift of the

Spirit. And the people are shaken. They're deeply moved, and not just because of Peter's words. While Peter's words are reaching their ears, the Spirit is reaching their hearts. (That's the way it always is. Words, without the grace of the Spirit, never converted anybody.)

"What should we do?" they ask.

"Each of you must turn away from his sins and be baptized," he tells them.

The word *repent* has a very deep meaning. Part of its meaning is that you must be willing to open up, be willing to change, to take a chance, to adventure toward God. Baptism will be a sign of this willingness to take up a whole new kind of life, if that's what God wants.

Throughout this scene we have God meeting people through people. That's the story of the church—the community of Christ's friends which now begins to spread. From the very beginning, people who have heard the Good News of Jesus' life, death, and resurrection and have responded in joy and faith have tended to come together to celebrate and live what they've come to believe.

So Pentecost isn't the end of the Jesus story, but the beginning. The coming of God among us and the pouring out of his Spirit was not a one-shot deal that happened a long time ago. It's a continual encounter that takes place not only in the individual human heart but within the community of those who, despite all their differences, are made one through their faith in Jesus Christ and remain faithful "to the teaching of the apostles, to the brotherhood, to the breaking of bread, and to the prayers."

The fire is still spreading. Do you feel it?

Things to Do

1. Have you ever heard news that was too good to believe?
2. Why was Thomas unwilling to accept the disciples' story of the Resurrection? Was his attitude unreasonable?
3. How can it be said that we who have never seen Jesus in the flesh are more fortunate than those who have?

4. What were some of the scripture passages that Jesus probably explained on the road to Emmaus?
5. How is Jesus' risen existence different from the life he knew before death? Does it tell us anything about ourselves?
6. If the two men had not invited the stranger to supper, they would have missed a vision of the risen Christ. Is Jesus trying to tell us something?
7. The whole Pentecost scene is so spectacular and so far removed from our everyday experience. What can it say to us about the life of the church as we know and experience it?
8. In the Gospel accounts and the Acts of the Apostles, trace the story of Peter before and after the coming of the Spirit. How does he change?
9. What message does Pentecost have for those who say they believe in Jesus but cannot find him in church?

PART THREE

GATHERINGS

14

Visions and Dreams

The Jesus story, as told in the New Testament, ends with Pentecost and the birth of the church. We are thus reminded that meeting Jesus Christ is not only an intensely personal, one-on-one encounter. It is something we do with others; we are all in this together. When Peter delivered his first great address that day, those who believed and came to faith did not walk home alone. They came together.

Those who accepted his message were baptized, and about three thousand persons were added that day. They devoted themselves to the teaching of the apostles and to the communal life, to the breaking of the bread and to the prayers.
All who believed were together and had all things in common; they would sell their property and possessions and divide them among all according to each one's need. Every day they devoted themselves to meeting together in the temple area and to breaking bread in their homes. They ate their meals with exultation and sincerity of heart, praising God and enjoying favor with all the people. And every day the Lord added to their number those who were being saved.—Acts 2:41-42, 44-47

This is how Christianity started: not as a random collection of individuals inspired by a common idea, but as a community. They came to faith together, cared for one another, and nourished one another's faith. They were deeply conscious of something that we Americans find difficult to grasp. They knew they belonged to Christ because they had been *called*. They saw their lives of faith as a free response to that call. This may seem obvious, but it is not. In our individualistic culture, most of us tend to think of ourselves as, at first, independent and unattached, then consciously choosing a religion and a church the way we choose products and clubs and jobs. That is not the way the church came into being. It is not the way we come to be part of the church. We have not chosen Christ; he has chosen us.

The early church was more than a movement, it was a living body. St. Paul calls it the Body of Christ, the living presence of Christ in the world.

Pentecost is a dynamic reality that calls for a personal response. It is not just a past happening, a spectacular episode which took place long ago and whose influence is felt today. Like the Gospel narratives we have been praying over, Pentecost is a process which is always *now*. Just as the events in Jesus' life are current realities in which we find ourselves personally involved, the coming of the Spirit is a divine manifestation addressed directly to us.

God entered the human condition in the person of Jesus Christ to encounter us and to enable us to encounter others. But the Incarnation did not end with the first century of our era. The Pentecost process flows from the Incarnation. But to comprehend what it means for us and for the whole world, we have to expand our minds and hearts.

Most people don't like to have their minds jarred. In the good old days, the sun and planets revolved around the earth. When Copernicus and Galileo put the earth in its rightful place, people didn't like it. No longer could everything be measured in terms of earth. In the same way, people prefer to measure all life in terms of their own lives. They assume that humankind is the highest form of life. So when a more exciting, intense, and dramatic life, the inner life of the Trinity, comes along, in some implicit way they resent it. "If I can't measure it with *my* ruler, it can't be that important." Yet, ironically, if people don't expand their minds and hearts to try in some small way to embrace the inner life of the Trinity, they will never understand how important they themselves are.

What is at the core of Pentecost? The heart of the matter is that we are swept up into the inner life of God, wherein we can encounter God and others. When we participate in God's life, we have the power to love God, to love others, to be loved. At the beginning of the Pentecost process, Peter proclaims that something shattering and profound has happened; that the fullness of time has come; that all people are called to decision; that the implications of that choice are tremendous. He reminds his hearers of the prophecy of Joel:

"It will come to pass in the last days,"
 God says,
 "that I will pour out a portion of my spirit
  upon all flesh.
Your sons and your daughters shall prophesy,
 your young men shall see visions,
 your old men shall dream dreams.
Indeed, upon my servants and my handmaids
 I will pour out a portion of my spirit in those days,
 and they shall prophesy.
And I will work wonders in the heavens above
 and signs on the earth below:
  blood, fire, and a cloud of smoke.
The sun shall be turned to darkness,
 and the moon to blood,
  before the coming of the great and
   splendid day of the Lord,
and it shall be that everyone shall be saved
  who calls on the name of the Lord."
      —Acts 2:17-21

When we open ourselves to the action of the Spirit and become part of the Pentecost process, we see visions and have dreams. We look at things differently and begin to live a different kind of life. When we become part of the community of disciples that is the church, we can have the same basic experiences that those first Christians did. This is not evident at first sight. It is hard for the casual reader to identify with them, for their situation seems utterly different from ours. But look more closely. What were they doing? They shared a vision, rejoiced and celebrated together, and took care of one another. They were not strangers to suffering and disappointment, but they found in their faith and in one another the strength to deal with them. The source of their security was no longer the things that they owned but rather the conviction that they were loved by God and by one another and would never be deserted by them. Their values had been changed; they had a new sense of what really counted. They saw others not as rivals or competitors but as members of a larger family with whom they wanted to share not only their belongings but also their newfound vision and deep-down joy.

This kind of thing still goes on today, and it can happen to us. At first sight, neither we nor the church as a whole looks much like the community of believers portrayed in the Acts of the Apostles. We are limited, sinful people, just as they were. But look more closely. People do care and make sacrifices for one another. Many an act of kindness or compassion or generosity is so routine as to be taken for granted, but God takes note. Whenever we respond to the needs of others and go that extra mile or even that extra step, we measure up a little better to our calling to be the Body of Christ. When we refuse to be part of political, economic, social, or even religious injustice and take a stand against systemic violence and exploitation, we bear witness to the action of Christ's Spirit in the world. And when we do these good things not only as individuals but together, mobilizing our resources and energies to make a difference in the lives of those around us and far away, the Pentecost process is happening here and now. We are acting as members of Christ's body, vitalized by the action of the Spirit. In ways large and small, we have become what Richard McBrien calls a model city, a "coming attraction" of the fullness of the kingdom.

Where do we get this power to love? From being swept up into God's life. The inner life of God is the most profound mystery. Keep in mind that God is one, but also three Persons.

Within the divine life there is an *I* and a *You;* the You is constantly meeting with the I. The I loves the You; the You loves the I. The I is interested in and shares all with the You; the You is interested in and shares all with the I. This meeting, this love between the I and the You, is so intense, so vivid and alive, that it is a person, the Holy Spirit.

Notice that the description of God's inner life and the description of love are the same. When scripture says that God is love, it's not just a nice poetic saying. It's reality.

God, the source of all love, is the source of your love for God, the source of your love for others, and the source of others' love for you.

Only if you participate in God's inner life can you have the power to love God. Only if you participate in God's inner life can you have the power to love others. Only then can you have the power to be loved.

Thanks to the fact that God became human, you are able to participate in the inner love life of God. Through Christ, you are swept up into this inner divine life, where you are able to encounter God and others. What do we call this Pentecost process of being swept up into God's inner life through Christ? We call it church.

This is the fullness of the Good News of Pentecost. Beneath the powerful symbols of wind, tongues of fire, charism, and conversion lies a deeper reality. Right here and now, the risen Christ shares with us the fulfillment of the basic heart wishes — to love, to be loved, to share, to blossom out. We will know this perfectly only after our own death and resurrection, but a foretaste beyond all imagining is possible in our immediate future, which begins today. In this Pentecost process called church you become one with Christ. This is no mere pious metaphor. In a mystical yet very real sense, you actually become Christ.

Imagine that you have a rich, famous, talented, wonderful friend who says to you, "My money is your money. Take as much as you want. My home is your home. I share my fame with you; now you will become as famous as I am. My talents, too, are yours; from now on, you are as talented and accomplished as I am. Even my inner life, my very self, I share with you. You and I are one."

This is what happens when you become one with Christ. God's joy, wisdom, peace, beauty, strength, courage, thoughts, attitudes, love experiences are no longer "up there" or "out there." You become one with God. Gradually God's joy becomes yours. Gradually you are filled with a wisdom, a peace, a beauty, a strength that is not your own. Gradually you experience a power to love and be loved—a power not your own. After a while you are no longer alone; you are one with God. Like any love encounter, this union grows, and like any love encounter, it is known only through experience.

And yet you must not imagine that, in becoming one with Christ, you lose your own identity. There has never been and never will be anyone quite like you. You are unique. Becoming one with Christ will not diminish your person and individuality. In fact, just the opposite happens. You become more you. The unique, real you will blossom forth as never before.

These passages in the New Testament will help you to understand how you become one with Christ. The first takes place in John's account of the Last Supper, when Jesus says to his followers:

"I am the true vine, and my Father is the vine grower. Remain in me, as I remain in you. Just as a branch cannot bear fruit on its own unless it remains on the vine, so neither can you unless you remain in me. I am the vine, you are the branches. Whoever remains in me and I in him will bear much fruit, because without me you can do nothing."—John 15:1, 4-5

In describing his relationship with us, Jesus calls himself a vine and us the branches. The vine and the branches are one, yet each branch is unique. Because of its union with the vine, the individual branch comes alive, grows, and blossoms.

Notice, too, that each branch, by virtue of its connection with the vine, is related to every other branch. Until now, in considering the process called church, you have studied only the union between you and Christ. If, however, you become one with Christ, and others become one with Christ, then, thanks to Christ, you and they are all united with one another.

This union called church is the work of Christ. His friends are brought together and swept up into his life. Like the union

VISIONS AND DREAMS   153

between Christ and you, the union between you and others continues to grow. Like any love relationship, the union is deepened and enriched by experience.

The second scripture passage that will help you understand your union with Christ is found in the Acts of the Apostles:

> Now Saul, still breathing murderous threats against the disciples of the Lord, went to the high priest and asked him for letters to the synagogues in Damascus, that, if he should find any men or women who belonged to the Way, he might bring them back to Jerusalem in chains. On his journey, as he was nearing Damascus, a light from the sky suddenly flashed around him. He fell to the ground and heard a voice saying to him, "Saul, Saul, why are you persecuting me?" He said, "Who are you, sir?" The reply came, "I am Jesus, whom you are persecuting. Now get up and go into the city and you will be told what you must do." — Acts 9:1-6

In the very early days of the church, the community of Christ's friends began to increase and aroused a persecution by the religious authorities. One of the most zealous persecutors of the Christians was Saul (later to be known as Paul), who made a series of arrests in Jerusalem and was on his way to Damascus to continue the persecution there.

Paul started out for Damascus as an enemy of Christ, but his experience on the road changed him forever. He arrived at Damascus as a friend of Christ; his conversion transformed him into a great missionary apostle, a towering figure in the church right up to our own day.

Notice Christ's words to Paul: "Why do you persecute *me?* . . . I am Jesus, whom you persecute."

Christ did not say to Paul, "Why do you persecute Christians?" or "Why do you persecute my friends?" but "Why do you persecute *me?*"

Christ is saying that he and the Christians are one.

Paul began to become aware of the depth of this wondrous truth that in the process called church, Christ and the Christian become one. Paul himself became a Christian and plunged into this process called church.

Years later, and many adventures and experiences later, Paul explained the process of church by using the example of the body:

> As a body is one though it has many parts, and all the parts of the body, though many, are one body, so also Christ. For in one Spirit we were all baptized into one body, whether Jews or Greeks, slaves or free persons, and we were all given to drink of one Spirit.
>
> Now the body is not a single part, but many. But as it is, there are many parts, yet one body. The eye cannot say to the hand, "I do not need you," nor again the head to the feet, "I do not need you." Indeed, the parts of the body that seem to be weaker are all the more necessary. If [one] part suffers, all the parts suffer with it; if one part is honored, all the parts share its joy. Now you are Christ's body, and individually parts of it. — 1 Corinthians 12:12-14, 20-22, 26-27

Paul sees church as being like a body. Christ is the head, and his friends are the parts of the body. Each member is unique, yet the head and the members are one.

Consider how close the head and members are! If you broke your arm and someone asked you how you felt, you wouldn't say, "I feel fine, not a care in the world. My arm hurts a lot, but I'm okay." When your arm hurts, *you* hurt! You and your arm are one.

If you get a bad infection in your leg, your whole body runs a fever. Your head, ears, eyes, hands, feet are all one. So also with Christ and his friends in the process called church.

If you have a problem, a sorrow, a hope, a joy, a fun thing, Christ has that problem, that sorrow, that hope, that joy, that fun thing along with you. You are not isolated and alone; Christ shares everything with you.

Conversely, every sorrow, hope, joy of Christ's is yours. Just as he shares your life, so you share his. When you think about it, this is an astounding idea, which takes a while to sink in. Only gradually will the implications begin to come clear. It means, for one thing, that all the scripture accounts concerning Christ in this book are living realities. You die with Christ; you rise with Christ. You can now read the Gospel events as part of your own biography!

So far you have considered how you and Christ share each other's life. Keep in mind that all the members of the body are related to one another. When you break your arm, you hurt. It's a problem for the whole body. An infection in your leg makes the whole body run a fever.

So it isn't just Christ who shares your hopes and joys and problems and sorrows and fun. The other members of Christ share them with you, too. Another member's joys or sorrows or hopes are yours, too.

This union among Christ's friends called church is brought about by Christ, who draws all together into his inner life and makes them one with himself. Like the union between Christ and you, this union between you and others grows and deepens through experience.

In summary, then:

- Pentecost is not just a past event, but a present reality.
- Pentecost is an ongoing process of being swept up into the inner life of God.
- Because God became human, you can participate in the inner life of God. Through Christ, you are swept up into this inner divine life.
- You encounter Christ in such a unique manner that you become one with him and yet become more the individual, interesting person you are meant to be.
- Just as you become one with Christ, so others become one with him and you become one with others.
- This is an ongoing process: The more you enter into God's inner love life through Christ, the more you will encounter God and others. This is what life is all about — love encounters with God and with others.
- This Pentecost process is called church.

Things to Do

1. What is the connection between Pentecost and church?
2. Do most people think of church as process? What image is more conventional? What difference does it make?
3. Have you ever felt that getting involved with Christianity might rob you of your individuality or diminish your personality? Why? How would you answer this objection?
4. Suppose we admit that union with Christ doesn't diminish your personality. Does Christ contribute anything positive to the real you? What?
5. For some people, the statements "You actually become Christ" and "You become one with God" are hard to swallow. Cite New Testament passages which try to explain these astounding notions. Explain them in your own words.
6. Name some experiences in your own life or the lives of others that illustrate this close union with Christ or with others in Christ.

15

Community and Conglomerate

When we throw in our lot with other believers and become part of Christ's church, we are challenged to keep a balance between two worlds, the ideal and the real.

On the one hand, the church embodies some of humankind's fondest hopes and highest ideals. It is called into being by God; it is mystery, the kingdom in germ, the Body of Christ. In this process called church, thanks to Christ, people enter into the inner love life of God and thus experience love encounters with God and others. We find support for our faith in the belief of others. We find strength for commitment when we see other Christians sticking it out through good times and bad. Our most generous impulses are affirmed, and the best parts of ourselves are called forth by our fellow disciples. We find that we are capable of so much more goodness than we thought. All these things can happen when we experience the church as community.

On the other hand, the church sometimes looks not like a community but more like a conglomerate. From time to time the church is undeniably human, wrongheaded, shortsighted, disappointing, and flawed. Some church members seem genuinely wicked and capable of doing vicious things to others. Some are not that bad but just don't seem to care about anyone but themselves. Others, though good and sincere, seem genuinely confused and can't figure out what life is all about. Others adore the "box," a nice, comfy, restricted little place that has its own little worldview which is neat and complete. Everything outside the box is measured by a ruler found inside the box, and nothing outside the box will "measure up." Some give lip service to new insights and breakthroughs but never really change; they just do business as usual. They are more interested in uniformity than in unity. Instead of channeling growth, they stunt it. They view options with suspicion. They prefer unequal distribution of power; they like it concentrated at the top.

Church as conglomerate is sometimes so painful that it tends to blur the image of church as community. This paradox is as old as the church itself. Even in the somewhat idealized descriptions of the early church in the Acts of the Apostles, all is not sweetness and light. There were disputes and power struggles from the very beginning, as well as cases of selfishness and betrayal. One of the reasons St. Paul has so many letters in the New Testament is that he periodically had to write to Christian communities in various cities to clear up misunderstandings, mediate quarrels, and settle arguments about the most basic beliefs and commitments.

Jesus himself, in the Gospels, makes it clear that he has no illusions about the people to whom he is entrusting his mission. They (we) are sinners who from time to time are sure to screw up. But some jobs are so important that they are worth doing, even badly. That's no excuse for slipshod work, but it should help us to have more realistic expectations. A church where everybody got along and never fought or disagreed about anything important or never had any collective problems sounds more like a club of fat cats than the church of Christ.

If we don't take this hopeful but hard-nosed approach, we are in danger of settling for one of two solutions when things go badly. Both are not real solutions but cop-outs. The first is to defend the church as conglomerate and say that since church as community is God's will, then church as conglomerate is God's will, too. The second is to admit that church as conglomerate is a mess, give up on the whole thing, including the church as community, and drop out.

There is a third way. It is based on an important and often overlooked aspect of the church, its capacity to grow and evolve.

Within the process called church, you and others, the community of Christ's friends, have this capacity to evolve. In growth by evolution, certain things happen:

- Part is gradually left behind (church as conglomerate situation).
- Part remains and evolves (church as community situation).
- There is a leap, an adventure, with all the scariness that this entails.
- Failures occur along the way.
- You realize that you cannot evolve without God and others.
- Things never happen in quite the way that you expect.
- Wonderful things beyond your imagination begin to happen.

Look at a seed and a flower. They are quite different, yet one comes from the other. You as a seventeen-year-old and you as a twenty-seven-year-old are quite different, yet one comes from the other. In the process called church, each of us is a transition person who is evolving into a goal person. The transition person is the person in present seed form; the goal person will be that person in future flower form.

transition	goal
seed	flower
myself now	myself as I will become
others now	others as they will become
God as experienced by me now	God as experienced by me in the future
community of Christ's friends now	community of Christ's friends as it will become

In the process called church, we must not try to pass the seed off as the flower. The seed is not the flower; it is on its way to becoming a flower.

What brings about this evolution in the process called church? There are two causes: God and the prophet.

GOD

God is gradually evolving the whole universe. Within this universe, God is daily occupied with evolving you, others, the community of Christ's friends, your ability to experience God and others in encounter, and the transition church into the goal church.

The process called church will not evolve on the strength of human endeavor alone. Although human effort is absolutely necessary, you can't expect to evolve without the evolver, God.

PROPHET

What do you think of when you hear the word *prophet?* Some fellow in a long, flowing robe. He's got to have a white beard. He's also going around predicting the future, so let's give him a crystal ball. Also, he's usually mad at the world. That's a prophet, right? Wrong!

The prophet is future oriented, but he or she doesn't have a crystal ball. The prophet is concerned with moving into the future. The prophet strives for an overview, cuts through to the heart of the matter. The prophet, aware of the evolutionary work of God, sees events in time as occasions to meet God.

Scratch the surface of a prophet and you find a mystic lover. At the prophet's heart of hearts is a love affair with God.

The prophet has plenty of problems, but they do not rob him or her of the deep-down joy whose source is God. Aware of being evolved by God, the prophet sees himself or herself as an evolver working together with God to bring the world and its people to the fulfillment of all their possibilities.

The prophet knows that God meets people through people, so in trying to reach others, he or she doesn't rely just on personal ability. The prophet lets the love of God flow through him or her to the other person.

The prophet is a people person who gives witness, through personal testimony, to what God and others mean to him or her.

But even then, the prophet is not so much a mouth as an ear—being attentive, listening, and only then speaking.

The prophet is never a loner, but is sometimes lonely. He or she needs to give and receive support. Often without realizing it, his or her own example is a strong motivating force for others. The prophet isn't a bionic person who leaps over buildings at a single bound, but, watching him or her, people get the feeling that some good things may be possible, after all.

Sometimes the prophet is an anxiety causer who makes waves. He or she goes around telling people that there is more to life than they think. This often makes people anxious and disturbed, for it upsets the status quo. People who get into a rut usually are comfortable and don't want to be told that there's something better and they're missing it. The prophet sees true happiness beyond the adventure, and in time others may see it, too.

When the prophet looks at the church, he or she sees more than the statistics would indicate. The prophet sees Christ loving each person in the world. When each person in turn goes out to others in love, the source of that love is Christ—whether that person knows it or not. Whenever people seek the good, the kind, the loving thing in life, they are seeking the source of love, kindness, goodness—Christ. The prophet sees all people tending toward Christ, even those who don't know him. The prophet sees the Holy Spirit at work throughout the world.

The prophet is community minded, public minded, world minded. Society's problems are the prophet's problems. He or she sees the church not as an escape or a fort, but rather as leaven, salt, sign.

The term *prophet* has been used here in a very wide sense. The prophet goes by many names: apostle, missioner, witness, God person, people person, God experiencer, people experiencer, lover, pioneer. The prophet can be called a *Christian.*

And here's the kicker: The prophet is you. You are prophet.

As prophet, you can help the church evolve into the model city it is meant to be. Together with other Christians, you can help the community of Christ's friends accomplish three fundamental and much-needed changes in its members and structures. Some of these changes may have to happen in you, too.

The first change that needs to be effected is in a way of

thinking, a basic mind-set. When some people reflect on religious realities, they think in static terms. Others think in process
categories. For the person with a static mind-set, the world is
complete. God's work of creation was finished a long time ago,
and it is our duty to preserve the order that has been built into
the world or to restore it when it has been disturbed. The
dynamic or process mentality, on the other hand, sees creation
as a continuing act still in progress and the world as not yet
complete. Our duty is to decide what direction we should move
in to realize our possibilities.

For the static thinker, the most important thing is to preserve
what already is, and the worst thing we can do is make a mistake.
For the process thinker, the most important thing is to probe
and explore, and the worst thing is not to try. As you can see,
these two ways of looking at the world create two very different
kinds of personality, two very different ways of judging and acting.

These divergent mind-sets have a great impact on the way
people relate to church. Both groups see themselves as the
guardians of tradition, but for the static thinker, the tradition is
a closed system. Innovation is suspect, and change is resented.
Loyalty and fidelity are conceived in narrow, rigid terms that
can stifle creativity and kill imagination before it is born.

Father Wes Seeliger, an Episcopal priest, pictures these two
mentalities as belonging to people in the Old West. He divides
Christians into two types: settlers and pioneers. For the settlers,
the church is a courthouse and God is the mayor of the town.
Jesus is the sheriff, and the settlers are a mayor-fearing people
who try to stay out of the sheriff's way. Faith is believing that
the mayor is in the courthouse and keeping the town's laws; sin
is breaking the laws. Salvation is hanging around the courthouse.

The pioneers, on the other hand, see the church as a covered
wagon where the pioneers live, love, fight, eat, and die. It is a
creaky, battle-scarred conveyance, always where the action is
and ready to explore the new world. God is the trail boss, full
of life and traveling with the people and sharing their hardships.
Jesus is the scout who rides ahead to find the way. Looking at
him, the pioneers figure out what pioneering really means. The
pioneers are daring, rugged adventurers who love the excitement

of life on the trail and feel sorry for the hidebound settlers. Faith is a readiness to "move out" in obedience to the voice of the restless trail boss. Salvation is trusting the trail boss and following the scout, and sin is wanting to turn back.

Settlers aren't bad people, but with their static mind-set they can get in the pioneers' way and keep them from doing what has to be done.

The second fundamental change to which prophets and pioneers call the church is to stop turning inward and to move outward in service to the world. Like all religious institutions, the church of Christ is subject to the occupational hazard of directing all or most of its energies and resources into self-preservation. Religious leaders can easily fall into this trap. Sometimes they feel so keenly the responsibility of caring for their people that they fear to take any risks. Like overprotective parents, they may try to shield their coreligionists from harmful contact with an unbelieving and mixed-up world. They can forget that the Christians they serve are adults, not children, and that they could not keep them from growing up even if they wanted to. There is also the temptation to take too literally Jesus' designation of them as shepherds of the flock, and mistakenly think of their people as sheep.

When religious leaders fall into these traps, they begin to behave in certain destructive ways that threaten the very institution they are trying to protect. They think of the people "under" them (a revealing metaphor!) as those to whom they must give orders but to whom they need not listen. An authoritarian style develops, and dissenting voices are either ignored or silenced. After a while, the only followers who listen are the few who really are afraid of growing up and are quite content to turn over to someone else the responsibility for decision and action. The grown-up members of the congregation are alienated and either become discouraged or leave altogether. At this point the metaphor of overprotective parents becomes all too apt, as the church begins to resemble those unhappy families in which growing children rebel against authoritarian rigidity.

These unhappy developments damage not only the church group but also the larger society that they are called to serve. Our world is torn by violence, selfishness, bigotry, and hunger (both physical and spiritual). It is in desperate need of inspiration, hope, and the good example of generous and responsible people. The church is admirably endowed to minister to these needs of the wider world. As disciples of Christ, we have so much to give! But in order to share the spiritual riches with which we have been blessed, we must be careful not to make the goal of all church activity the furthering of the institution's power and influence. In a world that is in danger of falling apart, and in a church that is beset by confusion and internal strife, this is like polishing brass on the *Titanic*.

The third change to which prophets must call the church grows out of the last one and is closely related to it. It is to resist all attempts at domesticating the Gospel. The message of Christ is a call to act justly not only in our personal lives, but also in our public lives. (Actually, it is a call to love, which is greater than justice, but let's take one thing at a time.) Christianity is not the only religion that has been used, from time to time, to lend an air of respectability to economic, political, and social structures that are inherently unjust. Some of the worst tyrants and most hypocritical rulers have draped themselves in the trappings of religiosity. This is scandalous enough, but they have also manipulated religious leaders and beguiled them into turning an occasional blind eye to their depredations.

Even in democratic nations that profess to respect basic rights and freedoms, there are always some long-standing arrangements that need to be called by their right names, denounced, and done away with. Those who criticize institutionalized wrongs can expect to incur resentment, but Jesus spoke out against every form of exploitation, and his followers must do no less. This is the very opposite of bland respectability. It can and usually does cost. There will always be voices of false prudence that will counsel caution and compromise and will predictably explain that the time is not right. They have never grasped the truth that, for evil to triumph, all that is needed is for good people to remain silent. Those who seriously profess to be followers of Jesus Christ must by their very vocation be activists for justice.

However, the church cannot be a credible prophetic voice if rights are violated and persons abused within the church itself.

When Jesus said that there would be scandals among his followers, he wasn't kidding. In a church of sinners, there will always be some people who play power games at the expense of truth and justice. History offers too many examples of violations of basic human rights, even at the highest levels of church administration. As Lord Acton once observed, all power corrupts, and all absolute power corrupts absolutely. There is a subtle form of self-deception at work here, for this kind of power is seldom used for personal gain but more often in the name of order or tradition or fidelity. People are mistreated in the name of love by those who do not understand that you cannot treat persons unjustly and still say that you love them.

We should not be shocked by these manifestations of sinfulness, but we are allowed, indeed encouraged, to be angry. Let it be the anger that Jesus showed when he drove the merchants out of the Temple. As with him, let our motive be not personal enmity but zeal for God's house. Let us work tirelessly for a church that not only preaches justice and love but practices them at home. And get ready for a long haul. This is one battle that won't be over until a few hours after the Second Coming of Christ.

Things to Do

1. Who are today's prophets?
2. Have you ever acted like a prophet? What happened?
3. Where do you see the static mind-set at work in the church?
4. Where do you see the process mind-set at work in the church?
5. What reforms are most needed in today's church?
6. Is the church capable of reform?

16

Who's in Charge Here?

The last chapter tried to deal realistically with the problems we face in becoming members of Christ's church. On the one hand, church membership offers us indispensable help in responding to the call to encounter God and our neighbor. We are not alone in these endeavors. On the other hand, it is a church of sinners that we join when we are baptized. This is a community that is always in need of reform and sometimes seems to bungle along and get in our way. We are encouraged to see the church as it really is, with its virtues and its failings, and to do our part to help it do better and play its role in the world with integrity and fidelity.

If we stopped there, we might be left with the impression that all the problems associated with church membership come from outdated structures or the misuse of power by church officials. As a matter of fact, some of the most intractable problems lie within ourselves. We, too, are sinners subject to all or most of the failings that were described. But even beyond our personal shortcomings are other factors that can create serious religious tensions. Certain characteristics of American culture pose formidable challenges to living out the Christian faith. All of us are immersed in this culture and are touched, even molded, by it in varying degrees. Two of the most pervasive and powerful influences that have serious implications for religious commitment are *individualism* and *consumerism*.

INDIVIDUALISM

One of the most striking characteristics of Americans noted by visitors to this country is individualism. Emile Durkheim, the great nineteenth-century sociologist, described the United States as a "giant collection of individual personalities." We are, by and large, rather proud of this national character trait. It accounts for much of what is distinctive and impressive about us as a people — our energy, our devotion to individual liberties, our love of freedom. We jealously guard our privacy and resist all movements that smack of collectivism. We are suspicious of indoctrination and insist on the right to form our own beliefs and make our own commitments. Authorities are tolerated only to the extent that they respect individual differences.

This value lies at the heart of the "great experiment," the inclusion of religious freedom in the Constitution of the newly founded United States of America. At the end of the eighteenth century, this decision to have no established church and allow a plurality of religions, or no religion, was a new idea. Contrary to the expectations of many, it worked, and worked so well that many modern states have borrowed it from us. It is certainly an enlightened way for government to deal with the differences among its citizens, and is one of America's finest exports to the world at large.

Although individualism protects people from those who would impose religious beliefs or practices on them, it does create some problems for those who want not only to be free of religious pressures but also to have positive religious convictions and share them with others in community. Before we describe these, however, it is important to distinguish individualism from individuality.

Individuality is that quality which distinguishes one person from another and gives that person a distinctive character. It is obviously a desirable trait. My individuality does not isolate me from others, but simply recognizes that I am a unique self and cannot be reduced to a type or a number or a function of a collective. Individuality enables me to have ideas of my own, to resist pressures to conform, to take responsibility for my own beliefs and commitments.

Individualism, on the other hand, is a doctrine or attitude which assumes that only the individual, and not society, is what counts. Individual initiative, action, and interests should be independent of social control. For this mentality, all values, rights, and duties originate only in individuals, not in the social whole.

If you think about it, you can see that individuality is quite compatible with religious faith and practice. As pointed out in chapter one, it is the characteristic that helps persons move from traditional to transitional faith. Individualism, on the other hand, does pose some real problems. At the very heart of Christianity is the conviction that we discover our deepest beliefs in and through tradition and community. But many Americans like to imagine themselves as completely autonomous, independent of any community or tradition, and then choosing a religion and a church. We like to think of ourselves as totally free, unshaped by outside influences, and finding within ourselves the roots of belief. This was strikingly demonstrated in a 1978 Gallup poll in which 80 percent of Americans agreed with the statement, "An individual should arrive at his or her own religious beliefs independent of any churches or synagogues." Anyone familiar with the American scene will not be surprised at this. But it is completely at odds with the traditional Christian and Jewish view of how we come to faith in response to a call from God within a community and mediated by a tradition. As Robert Bellah and his associates point out in *Habits of the Heart* (p. 227):

> This traditional pattern [is] hard for Americans to understand. The traditional pattern assumes a certain priority of the religious community over the individual. The community exists before the individual is born and will continue after his or her death. The relationship of the individual to God is ultimately personal, but is mediated by a whole pattern of community life. There is a givenness about the community and tradition. They are not normally a matter of individual choice.

We are reminded of the young woman referred to in chapter one who invented her own religion and named it after herself. She may seem an extreme example of religious individualism, but one wonders how unusual she is. There is a good deal of evidence to suggest that she may simply be doing, in a very explicit and articulate way, what many others do implicitly and even unconsciously. The notion of religious faith as a response to God's gratuitous revelation and our willingness to shape our beliefs and behavior in obedience to that revelation is hard to come by in our culture. Kenneth Briggs points out that:

> Americans are turning away from the dictates of organized religion and are drawing upon spiritual feelings of their own to define their faith, a leading researcher in religious values has found. Dr. William J. McCready, program director of the National Opinion Research Center at the University of Chicago, told a group of philanthropists that . . . for growing numbers of people an individual search for meaning has become the central religious experience.
>
> Many surveys have shown a declining influence of religious authorities on behavior. Dr. McCready said that because Americans had been powerfully imbued with the values of freedom and conscience, the pattern would probably continue.
>
> "Americans don't respond to moral imperatives," he said. "They increasingly behave any way they want to. They've been told to trust their consciences, and that's what they're doing" ("Religious Feeling Seen Strong in U.S.," New York *Times,* December 9, 1984).

There may be a mix of individuality and individualism here, but the latter seems to predominate. Especially revealing is the unwillingness to respond to moral imperatives. In the face of serious moral issues that confront us as a people, many Americans are unable to analyze the ethical content of those issues and simply resort to ritualistic slogans about how people shouldn't impose their morality on others. Underlying this kind of nonargument is a pervasive moral relativism, an unexamined assumption that "right" and "wrong" are just arbitrary labels, that no one really knows what is just and unjust, and that all morality resides only in the eye of the beholder.

This shows up quite often in religious contexts. When religious leaders denounce some conduct that they consider unjust and therefore sinful, they meet not only disagreement but also resentment. Disagreement is understandable, since people of good will can have their genuine disagreements, especially about problems that are sometimes complex and difficult to answer. But the resentment is something else, and has a certain edge to it. In some circles it is considered very bad form to tell anyone that they are doing something wrong. In fact, it is considered downright un-American. So when someone who is associated with a particular church, whether a leader or a member, objects to some behavior as unjust, this is considered an imposition of religion and a violation of the doctrine of separation of church and state. What began as a determination not to have an official state religion has ended up as an outlawing of moral discourse in the name of freedom of religion.

At this point some may say that this is an interesting analysis of unchurched people in our society, but what does it have to do with the people who are presumably serious about religion and are seeking a deepening of their religious faith? For many of them it is probably irrelevant, but surely not for all. Such a pervasive and deeply imbedded national trait is bound to have some effect on church members. McCready's research shows quite clearly that even within the churches, the religious quest is seen as an individual, not a communal, enterprise.

What practical impact does this have on a person's religious experience and practice? All Christians, even the most individualistic, agree that at the heart of their faith is the law of love. Jesus says that we are to love God and our neighbor. But what are the concrete demands of love? They are not always clear, and that is why we have moral controversies. Debates about such questions as euthanasia, sexual ethics, defense spending, abortion, nuclear weapons, human rights, capital punishment, and test-tube babies are rooted in disagreements about what justice and love demand in concrete situations. We are supposed to take these questions seriously and try to make correct moral judgments and decisions. For a Christian, that means trying to judge as God judges and acting as Christ would.

But how do we judge, and how do we decide? This is not the place for a detailed, technical treatment of the process of conscience formation, but this much can and must be said. We cannot simply look within ourselves, check our instincts and our feelings, and presume that we will infallibly make the right choices. Our instincts and feelings are important and should be listened to, but they are no guarantee of righteousness. We are all fallible, we all make mistakes, we are all subject to self-deception, especially in matters where we have something personal to gain or lose. That is why tradition is important. It is a standard against which we measure our private judgments. That is why we have church leaders, to help us find out what God is telling us through revelation and thus help us form a right conscience.

This may seem too obvious to need repeating, but it is not. Not only people outside the church, but also many of those within it, consider it an intrusion when their pastors offer moral guidance on contemporary issues. "Who are they to tell me what's right or wrong?" is a reaction that is becoming more and more common. "Why can't we just follow our conscience?"

Here are some statements by Catholic young people reacting to church teaching on premarital sex and abortion:

- God gave us life and told us he would not stand in the way, and would let us make our own decisions. Individuals should be the ones to dictate to themselves what their opinion on premarital sex is.
- The church can guide us, not tell us to say no, because the ultimate decision is ours alone.
- This is a free country. The church should be like a counselor who offers advice, and that's it. The government runs the country, not the church. I am a devout Christian who never misses Sunday Mass. When the priest uses the time for the homily to speak out on abortion, he is wrong. Priests are not politicians and have never had to worry about getting an abortion. They shouldn't be passing judgment on their neighbor. (I believe the Bible mentions that somewhere.)

If we are going to be members of Christ's church, we must understand what is the function of leaders within that church. They *have* to lead; it's their duty. It is a responsibility that they shirk at the risk of their souls. This is much easier to see when we look at the past. When we learn that in the recent past some church leaders failed to speak out on issues such as slavery and racial discrimination, we are shocked and ashamed. How, we wonder, could they have kept silent? Why didn't the churches come out more clearly for equality when American women were trying to win the right to vote? Where were the church leaders on the Pacific Coast in 1942 when, after Pearl Harbor, American citizens of Japanese descent were being interned in detention camps? Many other examples could be cited, but these should be enough to make the point that we rightly expect religious leaders to stand up for justice and human rights when these are being threatened or violated. Well, the same principles apply today. If God's children are being harmed by economic or political or social policies, by individuals or corporations or governments, the church is obliged to speak out. That goes for all members, and in a special way for those who bear the responsibility of exercising leadership.

Of course, those in authority are not always wise or always correct. Christians can and do disagree about the application of principles to difficult moral questions. The rank and file should be critical as well as open in their attitudes toward authoritative church teaching. Religious authorities cannot remove from their followers the burden of choice. There is such a thing as responsible, legitimate dissent. But the right to dissent has to be earned by study and prayer and dialogue. There is nothing infallible about the individual conscience, and the isolated individual is perhaps the most fallible of all. We all need help, and the church is supposed to provide that help.

Moral judgments and decisions are not the only aspects of religious life that are affected by individualism. The followers of Christ are called not only to justice but also to faith and to the expression of that faith in prayer and celebration. The church is not supposed to be a mere aggregate of isolated worshipers, another of Durkheim's gigantic collection of individual personalities. We are called to be a community, to nourish one another's faith, and to express that faith together in communal worship. The sacraments are privileged expressions of that worship, and the Eucharist is at the very heart of this people's love affair with God. This is no arbitrary regulation. We need one another, we need to be and to pray together, to hear God's word in solemn assembly, to gather at the Lord's table and eat the Bread of Life.

But the sacramental life of the church is not healthy, and the Eucharist is neglected. It is estimated that one-third of all Catholics in the United States rarely or never go to church, yet think of themselves as Catholics. We need not doubt their sincerity to be concerned. The empty pews on Sunday have many causes, including ignorance, laziness, and dissatisfaction (some of it justified) with the quality of liturgical celebration. But individualism has a lot to do with it, too. "Why do I have to go to church and put up with all those people, when I can stay home and pray to God all by myself?" So much is lost this way! But how can you even begin to explain it to them?

At any rate, it is good for us to be clear in our minds about the place of community in our relationship with God. Being a disciple of Christ is never a totally individual calling. It means throwing in our lot with a great many other people who are trying to do the same thing, some better than we and some not as well. Most people, at one time or another, find this part of Christian faith to be a nuisance, a burden, or even an obstacle. We can sometimes feel that going to God would be a lot easier without those other people getting in the way. But that's the way it is in all families. Even in the best of homes, people get on one another's nerves, create problems, and make life difficult for one another. But that's the price we pay to escape loneliness and share a life with those we love.

CONSUMERISM

The other aspect of American life that has a significant impact on our religious commitments is consumerism. Closely connected with individualism, consumerism is a reality so close to us that it can be hard to see. We have to step back a bit to put it in perspective. The dominant culture in our society encourages us to assess our worth purely in terms of the money we have and the things we buy. A meaningful life is reduced to grabbing, owning, enjoying, and consuming as conspicuously as possible in a hedonistic and materialistic vacuum. Advertising, Jean Kilbourne reminds us, is the propaganda of consumer society; it tells us who we are and what we should be. It tells us to be consumers; that products can fulfill us and satisfy our deepest human needs. This is a shallow and superficial vision of life that reduces it to a game in which the one who dies with the most toys wins. As we pointed out in chapter one, when people perceive its emptiness, they are moved to look for something more, and may find themselves reading a book like this one.

We like to think that we are not influenced by consumerism. Let's hope so. But it is hard to live in a society that uses powerful socializing forces such as advertising and the mass media and not be affected by their ubiquitous and insistent messages. Christianity is becoming more and more countercultural, based on an alternative vision of life whose aspirations are mocked by the voices of popular culture. The most powerful people in any society are not politicians, but the tellers of our stories and the singers of our songs. Every survey of the media elite — the women and men who write and produce the staples of popular entertainment — reveals that most of them have views on religion, marriage, sex, and success so different from ours that we must strike them as hopelessly superstitious, puritanical, and square. They have tuned us out, but can we tune them out? We have to try, but realism tells us that we may be affected by them more than we realize.

Is there a connection between consumerism and individualism? In the abstract, they are two different things. One defines us as consumers of products, the other as isolated selves without ties to community or tradition. In the concrete, they combine to create what James Fowler calls our culture's dominant myth: You should experience whatever you desire, own whatever you want, and relate intimately with whomever you wish (*Stages of Faith,* p. 20). This prescription for the Good Life is never explicitly spelled out. It is contained in thousands upon thousands of scripts, lyrics, and commercials, all the more effective for its implicit reinforcement of a taken-for-granted view of reality.

This worldview has implications diametrically opposed to the teachings of Christ.

The early converts to Christianity in the Roman Empire were faced with challenges strikingly like our own. Gentiles who were candidates for baptism had to undergo a rigorous examination and convince their sponsors that they were ready and willing to embark on a whole new way of life. The process was demanding, but it made a lot of sense. Roman society turned out Romans, and those who accepted uncritically the pagan values of their neighbors were not ready for membership in Christ's church. The countercultural character of the new faith was evident to the people of that time. It is only lately that we have come to see how much like theirs our own situation has become. As we consider the cost of discipleship, two of Jesus' parables speak eloquently to us:

> Whoever does not carry his own cross and come after me cannot be my disciple. Which of you wishing to construct a tower does not first sit down and calculate the cost to see if there is enough for its completion? Otherwise, after laying the foundation and finding himself unable to finish the work the onlookers should laugh at him and say, "This one began to build but did not have the resources to finish."
>
> Or what king marching into battle would not first sit down and decide whether with ten thousand troops he can successfully oppose another king advancing upon him with twenty thousand troops? But if not, while he is still far away, he will send a delegation to ask for peace terms. In the same way, everyone of you who does not renounce all his possessions cannot be my disciple. — Luke 14:27-33

If we are going to respond to the call of Christ and follow him in the believing and worshiping community called church, we must calculate the cost and ask ourselves if we have the resources and the will to pay the price. By ourselves, we cannot build the house or win the battle. But with God's help we can. The grace is there for the asking, and we must ask for it together.

Things to Do

1. What evidence of religious individualism have you observed in your own life or in those around you?
2. How have others been involved in the genesis of your faith?
3. Has your experience of church nourished your individuality, or has it been an obstacle?
4. Do you look to church leaders for help in making moral decisions?
5. Do you feel more comfortable praying alone or with others?
6. Do you see the dominant culture as a threat to your practice of the faith?

17

Special Meetings

In several ways during the last few chapters we have been insisting, in opposition to individualism, that religion is something we must do together. Therefore we have stressed the importance of tradition as part of our common story. The communitarian dimension of religious experience has, until recently in our history, been taken for granted in expressions of Judaism and Christianity. But powerful forces in today's culture make it difficult for us to be faithful to this dimension. Perhaps the strongest is privatization. This is the often taken-for-granted view that religion is a purely private affair, untouched by public issues and concerns and having no effect on public life. The assumption is that whatever answers I accept to the great questions about the meaning of life and about human destiny have nothing to do with my beliefs, attitudes, and practices in political, economic, and social affairs. In other words my relation to God is respected on condition that it is sealed off from the rest of my life.

We make headway against individualism and privatization, and we manage to assert our group identity in many ways, when we join in worship, when we work for common goals, when we build and support church-related institutions, when we speak out for justice, when we support social programs that serve the poor. Some of these activities have an explicitly religious flavor, others are implicit expressions of our Christian commitment to love and serve our neighbor.

There are certain key moments in our lives when our identity as members of the Body of Christ is expressed in special, powerful ways. We call these moments *sacraments*. All Christian churches recognize Baptism and Eucharist as sacraments; some communities have more. The Roman Catholic Church also recognizes Confirmation, Reconciliation, Anointing of the Sick, Holy Orders, and Matrimony. These rituals are often memorable, inspiring, and comforting. They can also be puzzling, pedestrian, and irritating. We live in a culture which is relatively impoverished in the matter of ritual celebration, so it is not surprising that we sometimes find it difficult to appreciate the sacramental expressions of our faith. So let us take another, closer look at these important moments in the Christian life, with particular attention to the so-called sacraments of initiation—Baptism, Confirmation, and Eucharist—and see how they can help us relate to and achieve union with God and others.

The first thing you must understand, if you are to appreciate the sacraments, is that they are occasions in which Jesus does for us now what he did long ago for the people he met when he first walked the earth. In the Gospel accounts we read of him forgiving sinners, feeding the hungry, healing the sick, and raising the dead. We tend to think of these as events limited to the distant past. But today we are forgiven our sins in the sacrament of Reconciliation. We eat the bread of life when we receive the Eucharist. The sacrament of Anointing of the Sick brings healing and comfort to us in times of serious illness or old age. And when we were baptized, we were born again to a new life. The same Jesus who was moved to compassion when he saw his people hungry or sick lives now, and he reacts the same way when he sees us in need.

At first sight these sacramental encounters may seem like pale reflections of those marvelous happenings long ago. After all, if thousands of people were fed with a few loaves and fish today, it would be front-page news. So would the miraculous cures of sick people. Even the TV soaps would be interrupted by news bulletins if someone were raised from the dead.

But look more closely. As impressive as the miracles were, the New Testament writers did not call them miracles but *signs*. Signs are used to point the way to something greater. The crowds who ate the loaves and fish were filled for a few hours but soon became hungry again. The day after, Jesus tells them (and us) not to hunger for ordinary bread, but for the bread that will give them life everlasting. The sick that he healed eventually became ill again. The dead whom he raised to life returned to the same mortal existence they had known before; they grew old, fell sick again, and died. But in the sacrament of Baptism, he raises us to a new, different kind of life — a life beyond the reach of weakness and stronger than death. So the marvelous events recounted in the Gospels were only pointing to greater realities in the here and now. They help us to understand what great things the Lord is doing for us.

People sometimes find it hard to appreciate sacraments because they think of them as mere ceremonies. But Catholic theology reminds us that these ritual signs, these actions that employ water, bread, wine, oil, and gestures, are *efficacious* signs. They actually accomplish what they signify. The consecrated bread and wine in the Eucharistic celebration do not merely symbolize Christ's flesh and blood, they really become him, and we really receive him in Holy Communion. The water used in Baptism does not merely stand for new life; we are really born again and receive a share of God's life. When the priest says the words of absolution in the sacrament of Reconciliation, our sins are truly wiped away.

Still, we must not think of these sacraments as if they were a kind of magic. God truly works in our lives, but not without our consent. Sacraments are encounters with Christ, special occasions when we open ourselves in faith to God's gracious action in our regard. This is true whether we receive the Eucharist, ask pardon for our sins, seal our Christian marriage, or accept the mission of Holy Orders. These meetings bring us closer to God and to one another. They give us strength for the journey of life. They not only enrich us individually but they also help us build up the Body of Christ which is the church. For while sacraments are, in a real sense, one-on-one encounters with Christ, they are not individualistic religious activities but actions of the community that are meant to bring us together.

INITIATION

Baptism is the first sacrament, the moment of our first meeting with Christ. In the first decades of the church's existence,

Confirmation was probably not considered a distinct sacrament. But when the practice of infant Baptism became common, the special anointing with the Holy Spirit that was part of the adult initiation rite was postponed until a later date, just as the reception of Holy Communion was delayed until the child was older and could understand. The three sacraments were thought of as parts of one initiation, and when adults are received into the church today, they receive all three together.

Many people have a very limited understanding of Baptism. Ask them what the sacrament does, and they will say it removes original sin. One can make a case for this kind of language, but the fixation of removing sin misses by a wide margin the heart of the rite, which is the bestowal of a new life and the making of a new member of the church. Most of us were brought into the church as infants, so the commitment to a Christian life was made for us by our parents. When we become adults, it is up to us to respond to Christ's invitation, to accept the faith given us, and to live as disciples of Christ.

The day you were baptized, you and Christ met for the first time. You entered into his life, and he entered into yours. Ever since then, whether you realized it or not, you have never been completely alone. Even at those times when you felt utterly isolated, he was there. Do you have a problem? The problem is his as well as yours. Do you have a hope for the future? You and Christ are hoping together. Do you experience a joy? You and he are happy together. At work, on the train, at the party, in front of the TV set—you and Christ share it all.

Love seeks union. A mother wants to hug her baby, and even the baby instinctively opens his or her arms to be hugged. A girl and a boy want to embrace each other. Lovers want to be close, and Baptism is a first embrace of love. Once you enter into Christ's life, God's joy, wisdom, peace, beauty, strength, and love experiences are no longer "over there." You are part of them. God is no longer "up there" or "out there." You are one with God. Since you became one with Christ at Baptism, you have been endowed with a wisdom, a peace, a beauty, a strength that are not your own.

But that's not all. In encountering you, Christ brings about an encounter with others. Just as you become one with Christ, so others become one with him. Thanks to him, you become one with each other. In this union among Christ's friends called church, you are swept up into Christ's inner life and thus brought together. Now when you have a problem or a joy or a sorrow or a hope, you share it with other members of Christ, and they share their experiences with you.

This union, sharing, and encounter are not based on human ability alone. More happens than what the parties concerned can bring about. This is what we call a twenty-pound love situation. You put five pounds of love into a situation, and the other person responds with five pounds. What ought to add up to a ten-pound love situation actually results in twenty pounds of love. How come? Well, more is happening there than the two parties can contribute; a third party—Christ—is present, so a twenty-pound love situation results.

Christ causes and increases the chemistry of your human encounters. Christ cooperates with you in providential meetings with others. He helps you in the difficulties that accompany every serious relationship. He gradually brings about encounter, in its fullest meaning, between you and others. This includes being receptive to communication, reaching out to others, sharing in their emotions and experiences, desiring to make others happy, and knowing that others desire to make you happy. Thus you grow in your capacity to love and be loved.

This capacity helps you deal with the challenges that come with growth and maturity. When the first glow of intimacy and romance wears off, we have to come to terms with our own shortcomings and the limitations of others. We have to carry the burdens that come with responsibility for those we love. Sometimes those burdens seem too heavy to bear by ourselves. That is when Christ is at your side, ready to help, offering you the strength to get through another day without betraying yourself or those close to you.

With his help, more is available to us than lives of quiet desperation. When you open yourself to his grace, your relationships with God and others can deepen in ways that will surprise you. And there's more. Your world will expand, and so will your hopes and fears and concerns. When you join God's family, all women and men become your sisters and brothers, and you become aware of your responsibility for one another. Just as Jesus had a special care for the poor and the outcast, you find yourself more and more preoccupied with the victims of poverty and injustice, wherever they may be. You can no longer be satisfied if you, your family, friends, and associates are comfortable and secure. As the circle of your concern widens, neglect and injustice, under whatever guise, become intolerable. You find that you have joined the human race and belong in a way that you never did before. And though restlessness has robbed you of your complacency, it has, in a deeper sense, made you more alive.

RECEIVING THE SPIRIT

Several years ago, archaeologists discovered the resting place of a mummy that was more than 2,500 years old. When they opened it, they found some seeds interred with the mummy. On being exposed to the air, these seeds, which had lain dormant for over two millennia, proceeded to sprout and grow.

The memory of your Confirmation day is probably very hazy by now. It's hard to think of anything that happened at that time of your life as being very significant. But at that second stage of your initiation into God's family, you encountered Christ and received the Holy Spirit in a very special way. For many of us, the effects of this encounter and action of the Spirit, like the Egyptian seeds, may lie dormant for a long time before they blossom forth in our lives.

Perhaps the best name for the Holy Spirit is the Enabler. The Spirit enables you to encounter God and others. Love encounters are what your life is all about — encounters that are one-on-one, tender, in some way exclusive, and yet overflowing into love for others. The Spirit helps make these wonderful encounters happen in your life. Christian tradition calls these actions the gifts of the Holy Spirit: knowledge, understanding, piety, wisdom, counsel, fortitude, and fear of the Lord.

The gift of knowledge puts you, in the deepest sense, in touch with the universe. You are able to look at nature and see God. At first you see the things of nature as beautiful in themselves, without reference to the God who made them. When you begin to see them as gifts from God—visible symbols of an invisible love—a whole new dimension of creation opens for you, and you perceive not only its beauty, but the source of all its wonder—the bountiful hand of God.

The gift of understanding helps you know God in a personally meaningful way. In your childhood and teenage years, you may have accumulated religious information about God, Christ, and the church. Thanks to the Spirit, this information can come together and take on a deeper meaning. Rather than just knowing with your mind, you *experience* God. This may happen when you are praying, reading, listening, or doing almost anything, and it may happen at any stage of your life. Some seeds take longer than others to blossom into life.

"I have much more to tell you, but you cannot bear it now. But when he comes, the Spirit of truth, he will guide you to all truth. I have told you this while I am with you. The Advocate, the holy Spirit that the Father will send in my name—he will teach you everything and remind you of all that [I] told you."—John 16:12, 13; 14:25, 26

Another gift that helps you reach even higher degrees of intimacy with God and others is called piety. For some, this word is burdened with a rather negative image, but it stands for something very beautiful. Thanks to the encounter between you and the Spirit, prayer becomes less of a ceremony and more of a meeting between persons. You find yourself wanting to pray, open to new experiences and to the influence of the Spirit. You become open to different forms of prayer as the Spirit prays through you.

Ideally, prayer should always be a deep and emotional experience, but of course it is not. Sometimes our mood is blah, we don't feel like praying, yet we want to. That inner desire comes from the Spirit.

Prayer can be an encounter not only with God, but also with the person you love. Usually when people tell someone they will pray for them, they mean something like this: "I will send telegrams to heaven on your behalf." This is fine, but an even deeper experience is possible. The Spirit helps you see prayer not only as an intercession for the other, but also as an encounter *with* the other. When you pray with someone, the meeting is more than just being together in the same place sending messages on each other's behalf. If you are open to it, the Spirit can bring about an encounter between you and the other with whom you are praying. This can happen even though you may be miles away, on the other side of the globe, or praying at different times. The Spirit is not limited by space or time and can make you present to each other at a most profound level. So when distance and time separate you from someone dear to you, you can agree not only to pray for each other but to meet in prayer.

Wisdom, despite its traditional name, has nothing to do with being smart. Rather, it is the gift that makes intimacy with God possible.

It's like the difference between hearing or reading about a show and actually seeing it. You read in today's paper that a certain program will be on television. Now you know about the program, and you may even read a critic's review; but you haven't experienced it. That won't happen until this evening. Similarly, we can hear about God, study about God, and, to a certain extent, know about God without ever having really experienced God. The Holy Spirit will bring about an intimate encounter with God, if you but ask.

God, please reveal yourself to me. What are you really like? Will the real God please stand up? What are your thoughts, your feelings, your experiences? What do you think of yourself? What is your attitude toward yourself? The philosopher tells me that you are the source of truth and goodness and beauty and love and life. That statement means nothing to me. I want to experience your goodness, your beauty, your truth, your love, your life. God, please reveal yourself to me, and continue to do so.

When you accept the gift of wisdom from the Spirit, your prayer is answered, and you know it.

These gifts of knowledge, understanding, piety, and wisdom make encounters with God on deeper and deeper levels of intimacy possible. Yet the Spirit does not stop there. In the divine plan, your encounter with God is oriented toward action. Real love between two people, far from narrowing their world, helps them move beyond their relationship, to others.

A relationship is like a pebble which, dropped in a pool of water, sends out ever-widening ripples. The Spirit helps you meet God in helping you go out to others, too, through gifts that are traditionally called counsel, fortitude, and fear of the Lord.

The gift of counsel helps you discern the ways that lead to God. No matter how earnest or open we are, all of us are confronted, from time to time, with complex problems and difficult decisions. "What should I do in this concrete situation here and now?" "What shall I do in regard to this person?" "How do I handle this hope for the future?" "What do I really want?" Here is where the Holy Spirit comes to help. "I will ask the Father, and he will give you another Advocate to be with you always, the Spirit of truth, which the world cannot accept, because it neither sees nor knows it. But you know it, because it remains with you, and will be in you" (John 14:16, 17).

The gift of fortitude gives you a courage that is more than your own, the courage of the Spirit. A law of life says that beyond the adventure lies true happiness. Thanks to the Spirit, the adventure is not so fearful. Some interesting changes come over you. You become willing to talk about Christ, to give personal witness to what has happened between him and you. You become more willing to support others as they endeavor to encounter Christ and others.

> Do not let your hearts be troubled or afraid. You heard me tell you, "I am going away and I will come back to you." When the Advocate comes whom I will send you from the Father, the Spirit of truth that proceeds from the Father, he will testify to me. And you also testify, because you have been with me from the beginning. — John 14:27, 28; 15:26, 27

The fear of the Lord is a gift whose name may put some off because it seems to imply threats or intimidation. But scripture tells us, "The fear of the Lord is the beginning of wisdom" (Psalms 111:10). It helps us realize what it means to be a creature before God. We come to know—not in theory, but from experience—that we cannot do it all by ourselves; that without a deep personal encounter with God, our own strength and insights are not sufficient. "I can't do it alone" isn't mere lip service; it's an intuitional experience brought about by the Holy Spirit.

Of course these gifts, for all their richness, do not exhaust the action of the Spirit. Every impulse, every movement, every encounter between you and God is a manifestation of the Spirit at work within you. But this traditional catalog of grace-filled experiences does help us have some idea, however inadequate, of the great things that the Enabler does for us.

OPEN TO THE SPIRIT

Confirmation as a ceremony happens only once, but Christ, the Encounter Causer of your future, promises to give you the Spirit every day for the rest of your life. To put it simply, you are being confirmed every day. Because of Confirmation, the Spirit is always present to you. The question is: Are you open to the Spirit?

Try to be open and ready to receive the Holy Spirit. Remember that the Spirit's action is a manifestation of God's love for you and for others. God wants you not only to receive this love but to pass it on to others, too.

God doesn't want you to be a Dead Sea Christian. The Dead Sea in Palestine is a unique body of water located at the lowest point on the surface of the earth. Rivers flow into it, but nothing flows out. It receives but doesn't give. As a result, the minerals and salt that flow in have accumulated to such a degree that there is no life at all in that vast body of water. Normally in a lake, water flows in and water flows out; that's why it lives.

Some people seem to become Dead Sea or "dead end" Christians. They receive love from God and insights into the meaning of life, but they give nothing, so they begin to die inside.

In giving, remember one thing: If you share with another what you have received, if you talk to another about the meaning of life, if you do some act of love for another—don't rely just on your own ability or your own love. Your words can reach only that person's ears, but if you let God's influence flow through you, you may reach the hot button in their heart. So when you act out of love for others, let God's love flow through you.

Who are those others with whom you are called to share God's gifts? People close to you, of course. Friends and associates, those with whom you are involved from day to day, and members of your community. But the Spirit may be prompting you to widen that circle, to include people who can easily be invisible and escape your concern. The poor, the powerless, the oppressed are both far away and close at hand. It is all too easy to forget or ignore these people at the margins of our world. All kinds of arrangements, some outside us and some within us, conspire to crowd them out of our consciousness. If we listen closely, we will hear the Spirit gently but insistently reminding us to look, to care, to act in whatever way we can.

Maybe you've been doing this sort of thing for the past few years. If so, it's a sign that the gift of the Spirit has enriched your life and the lives of those around you.

If you haven't been living this way, if your record so far resembles that of the Dead Sea, don't be discouraged. If Egyptian seeds can sprout after two thousand years, then the seed that God sowed on your Confirmation day is just waiting to burst into life.

Things to Do

1. Jesus Christ is separated from us by nineteen centuries, by differences in language, culture, and mentality. How does he bridge the gap between himself and us?
2. George Washington and Abraham Lincoln live on in the minds and hearts of Americans and still inspire us by their words and example. Is this what Christians mean when they say that Christ lives today?
3. Throughout this chapter the authors have stressed that sacraments are not *things* but encounters. What difference does it make?
4. Has your idea of piety changed over the years? How?

5. Have you ever been physically distant from someone you love and still felt close to that person? Describe the circumstances.
6. Can you remember an experience when either you knew or now realize that the Spirit helped you?

18

Ceremonies and Events

Imagine that it is your wedding day. And what a day! Rain is coming down in buckets. You wake up with a severe cold; your head is stuffed, and your nose is running. Because of the downpour, most of the people arrive at the church late, confused, and upset. When it's time to begin, there's no sign of the organist. The woman who fills in during the emergency attacks the organ as if she were wearing boxing gloves.

Half the lights in the church don't work. Your nose keeps running. Two dogs decide to fight just outside the window. As you leave the church, you meet some of your dearest friends just arriving; they had been held up by the weather. And to put the icing on the cake, a passing car splashes mud all over you.

Most likely it will take some time before you calm down and the tremendous realization sets in. Though the ceremony was awful, something wonderful happened: You were married to the person you love. God brought you together as husband and wife. By God's power, you are united to share each other's lives.

The wedding *as ceremony* was a disaster. It couldn't have been worse. The wedding *as event,* however, was a different story. In spite of all the mishaps, something wonderful happened. You chose each other. God joined you together. Not only that. Because of the wedding, many more wonderful things will happen in the future. The best is yet to come.

Because the event is so important, people are careful to make the wedding a beautiful ceremony. But if, for one reason or another, things don't go as planned, people aren't too disappointed. They know that underneath a poor ceremony, a most significant event has taken place, and that's what really matters.

The same is true of the Eucharist, the third of the sacraments of initiation and the celebration at the very heart of the Christian life. Because Christ's sacrifice is so important and so wonderful, people rightly insist that it should be celebrated in a beautiful and inspiring way. The Eucharist deserves the very best that we can bring to it. But even when everyone does their best, failure is possible. People are imperfect, and sincere efforts sometimes yield uneven results. Everyone wants the celebration to be a deep, emotional experience, but it will not always be enjoyable and inspiring. Just to list the reasons, even without discussing them, would fill a book.

Although it may seem dull or boring on the surface, much more than we realize is happening, not only during, but after the liturgical action. If we lose sight of the Mass as the celebration of a sacramental event, we may begin to evaluate it purely in terms of the immediate emotional return on our investment of time and effort. Thus we remember celebrations in which everything came together—a sense of community, an inspiring homily, a feeling of palpable personal enrichment—and we rightly esteem them as meaningful religious experiences. But when these desirable outcomes don't take place—when the hour drags, the celebrant is plodding, and the group is unresponsive— we are tempted to dismiss the whole experience as worthless. "I didn't get anything out of it." This is an understandable but mistaken reaction. We are right to be disappointed, and we should all resolve to try our best to do better next time. But we must get beneath the surface if we are to have a proper understanding and appreciation of the Eucharist.

A PLAY IN TWO ACTS

To understand what is happening, it helps to picture the structure of the liturgy. Too often a person at Mass perceives only a random succession of prayers, gestures, and actions—a confusing jumble with no apparent order or cohesion. To dispel some of the confusion and shed some light, think of the Mass as a drama in two acts, each with two scenes:

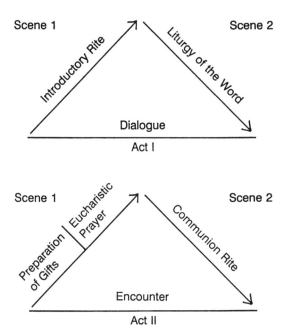

Act I, Scene 1: Introductory Rite. Christ is very much present in the first scene of Act I, the dialogue part of the Mass. He brings and holds the worshipers together in the community prayers of the Introductory Rite. Here we respond to Christ's invitation and come to God's house. We acknowledge our failings and weaknesses and ask for help in our efforts to do better.

Act I, Scene 2: Liturgy of the Word. If you see the scripture in the dialogue part of the Mass as merely a set of readings from a 2,000-year-old book, you've missed the point. Rather, it is God present and speaking to you through the living word of the scriptures. The readings and the homily are God's opportunity to speak to you in a special way, to tell you what is important, to offer you inspiration and encouragement and advice on how to live. They give people a chance not only to talk to God but to listen, to get God's slant on things, and, if necessary, to get help to change.

Act II, Scene 1: Preparation of the Gifts; Eucharistic Prayer. The second or encounter part of the liturgy begins with the preparation of gifts, as bread and wine are placed on the altar. These are symbols of all that occurs in life—work, play, joy, sorrow, hope.

In the Eucharistic prayer, the priest tells once again the story of the Last Supper, the suffering and death of Jesus on the cross, and his glorious resurrection from the dead and ascension into heaven. But this is not just a recital of a long-ago event. At the climactic moment of the words of consecration, the bread and wine become the body and blood of Jesus Christ present upon the altar. In a mysterious but profoundly true sense, his saving death and resurrection are made present and at work among us. Christ, risen from the dead and living today, transcends the limitations of time and space. He makes effective in the present an event of the past.

Your life and Christ's life thus become one. Your life and the lives of all those at Mass merge, as well as those at a distance, even on the other side of the world. And so his life, your life, and the lives of others become one. Christ gathers all these lives and places them in the hands of the Father. Thus we have the beginning of encounter in the Mass event. When you give yourself to God, you give a life that has been united with the life of Christ and the lives of others.

Act II, Scene 2: Communion Rite. Encounter in the liturgy continues. God is not to be outdone. Just as you gave yourself to God, so now you receive God in Holy Communion. You intimately meet Christ, who gives himself, body and blood, in his entirety, to you. He holds nothing back.

And he doesn't stop there. In Communion he brings about a meeting between you and others: with those at Mass here and now, and with those far away. Even if someone you love is at a distance and attending Mass at another time, Christ can make you both present to each other.

ASKING THE RIGHT QUESTIONS

This is what's really happening during that hour when Christians meet to celebrate Jesus Christ's victory over sin and death.

Until you search beneath the ceremony of the Eucharist to the event, not only will you come up with the wrong answers about the Mass, but you won't even ask the right questions.

"Why go to Mass? What do I get out of it? Is it a sin if I don't go? Why put up with boredom?" As long as you ask these questions and look for answers only in how you feel during the liturgy, as long as you stay on the level of the external ceremony and its immediate impact on your emotions, you're going to miss the whole point. Instead, you must ask, "What's happening at Mass? Who's there? What is the mystery beneath the surface, and how can it touch my life?"

The answers to these questions can put you in touch with Christ. All the experiences of Christ's life become yours. Every adventure, every problem, sorrow, hope, or joy that Jesus experienced is now yours. All the stories about him in the New Testament are realities in your life. You live with Christ, you die with him, and you rise with him. You bring with you your struggles, your weakness, your fears, and even your failures. He gives you the strength to bear and overcome them or just keep on trying. You also bring all your goodness: the unselfishness, the acts of generosity, the courage, the sacrifices, and all the other ways, great and small, in which grace has triumphed in your life. He celebrates them with you. And so God's joy, wisdom, peace, beauty, strength, courage, thoughts, attitudes, and love experiences gradually become yours. In the Mass event, you become one with Christ.

When you receive Christ's body into your body, you are receiving a promise from him. He pledges to you, with his own body, that he will bring your body to perfection in your own risen life. This God who comes to you in Holy Communion is not a threatening God, but one who is aware of people's feelings of being constantly manipulated, cramped, absorbed. Here is the highest form of life coming to you under the appearance of bread.

Finally, and this is most important, remember that in the Eucharist you are meeting with Christ, the encounter causer of your future. As a result, the wonderful things described here reach beyond the actual time of the liturgy. Christ can bring these about in the hours and days following the Mass, if you leave yourself open to the experience.

On Sunday morning during the liturgy, you meet with Christ, the encounter causer of your future. Maybe you are sleepy, or feeling blah. "I met with Christ, the encounter causer of my future. So what?" you say. On Wednesday, something wonderful takes place between you and him. "That's what!" says Christ. Don't limit the consequences of the Eucharist to the hour of Mass. Leave yourself open. He wants to encounter you and share God's life with you in an astonishingly intimate way. And this can make a tremendous difference in your life. The results of the Eucharistic action are profound, and they take place between you and Christ, between you and others, both now and in the future.

BETWEEN YOU AND CHRIST

Your giving of yourself to Christ and his gift of himself to you have love-encounter consequences. When you have a problem, a sorrow, a joy, or when you experience loneliness, confusion, or hope, Christ shares that problem, that sorrow, that joy, that loneliness, that confusion, that hope, with you. Laughter, tears, rush and bother, emptiness of heart, a sudden insight, the longing for something better—you are not alone in these experiences. Christ shares them with you. Conversely, all the experiences of Christ's life now become yours. Every adventure, every sorrow, hope, and joy that Christ experienced are now part of your story. You and he have become one, and this Mass event is a time to celebrate that wonderful reality.

You need this kind of celebration, because God is not always experienced as perfect and caring. To your limited perception, God sometimes seems hidden, uninterested, and distant. God seems to let you down. But the Eucharist is a reminder of how much God loves you and is constantly doing for you.

You also need this celebration because sometimes your perception of yourself is limited. There is so much more going on in our lives than we are aware of! Our efforts to live Christ-centered lives of faith and justice are of great price and value in God's sight. We may miss the drama in our own story, but

God does not. Mass is a time when we can hear, a little more distinctly, the inner music of life lived in response to the Gospel.

People often respond to these love actions with nothing more than "sponge" gratitude or with "balancing-the-books" gratitude. "Sponge" gratitude is really ingratitude. They just absorb God's gifts and go their merry way without ever acknowledging them. "Balancing-the-books" gratitude isn't much better. They thank God, but merely to straighten their accounts. They don't like the idea of anyone, even God, being one up on them.

What, then, is true gratitude? To answer, you must first understand what a gift is. It is a symbol of love. People can't see love, so they use symbols. For example, a wedding ring is a symbol of the love between husband and wife. In giving you a gift, God is saying, "Here, I want you to have this. Enjoy it. See it as a symbol of my love for you." The gift is a symbol of love, and true gratitude is the return of love for love received.

Now look at the Eucharist again. In the Mass, Christ's life and yours are united. As a result, the gratitude you give to God is infinite. For although you are limited, your life is fused with Christ's, so that your gratitude for God's gifts literally knows no bounds. In a real sense, you can meet God in an "equal" return of love for love received.

Of course, your relationship to God is one of creature to creator, and hence "uphill." But, thanks to the Mass event, you can meet God face-to-face as an "equal." And that's important. For a love relationship to be deep, the two persons must be able, in some sense, to meet as equals. The same is true of your relationship with God. Through the Eucharist, even this is possible.

BETWEEN YOU AND OTHERS

We have considered the love encounters between you and Christ. Now let's look at the love encounters between you and others. Just as you and he meet in the Mass, so he meets others, and, thanks to him, you and they encounter one another. Since Christ brings about this meeting between you and others, more happens than either you or others could bring about. He initiates and increases the depths of these encounters. Your capacity to love and to be loved is increased. Thus you have the potential for the most intimate encounters possible.

Moreover, these encounters are possible, not only with those in your immediate circle, but also with those at a distance, even with those on the other side of the globe — in fact, with everyone in the world. All your work, joys, longings, sorrows, and strivings are now shared by others. You are no longer alone. The joys and sorrows and hopes and longings of others are now shared by you.

What is the result of all this? Well, suppose you're reading a newspaper or watching the TV news. There is a report of mass starvation among the people of a remote country. If you're not careful, you find yourself beginning to think, "Those people are supposed to starve. They've always been starving; they always will starve. That's the way it is."

Or suppose a person or a family, here or abroad, is suffering. Again the mind-set begins to form: "Those people have always been sick or lonely or have suffered loss. That's just the way it is."

But that isn't just the way it is. Not anymore. Those problems of sickness, loneliness, loss, or starvation are now part of *your* life picture. You met these people in the Mass event. No matter what their color, age, religion, or place on the globe, thanks to the Mass encounter, your lives are one. You are all one with Christ, members of his body, and when they hurt, you feel it.

As a result, justice, peace, service, and development are not fringe activities of Christianity, optional for those who are into that sort of thing. They are central to the Eucharistic encounter; they are at the heart of Christian life.

Christianity is not just a philosophy, a system of ethics. Christianity is a call to action, a summons to help the poor, the suffering, the oppressed. Christians answer the call in many different ways: by collecting money or clothes for the poor, by visiting the sick, by listening to someone with a problem, by being with someone who is lonely, or by feeding handicapped kids in a nearby hospital. Christians may try to get at the root of some social or economic problem. They may just be available, or they may throw a party at a nursing home to bring help and a little fun, too.

If Christians are going to be church the way Jesus wanted, there must be a real sense of belonging. Each person's problem is everyone's problem. Your hopes are their hopes, too. Get to know each other, pray together, work together, have fun together. It's nice to know you have friends all over the place. Though far from perfect, all belong to one another because all belong to Christ in this community called church.

The church is a community, but it is not a fort. It is not a place to escape from the world, to flee from society, to crawl into and pull up the drawbridge.

"You are the salt of the earth. But if salt loses its taste, with what can it be seasoned? It is no longer good for anything but to be thrown out and trampled underfoot. You are the light of the world. A city set on a mountain cannot be hidden. Nor do they light a lamp and then put it under a bushel basket; it is set on a lampstand, where it gives light to all in the house. Just so, your light must shine before others, that they may see your good deeds and glorify your heavenly Father." — Matthew 5:13-16

If you've ever been lost, you know how it feels to finally spot a sign with a big arrow that points to where you want to go. The church of Christ is a sign, an arrow. It tells society, "This is the way. Here's where the action is."

Action, whether social, educational, financial, political, or economic, varies with time and place and the needs of society. The action may be organizational, like forming a credit union, or individual, like talking to a kid in school whom everyone else rejects. Big and small, social and private — all are necessary.

The Christian sees a need in society, rolls up his or her sleeves, and pitches in. This isn't the end of the story. The church also points out the needs to society at large and urges all people of good will to join in the action. Only then is the community the salt of the earth, the city on the hill, the light that shines before the world.

The Mass is the center and source of the action. The Mass is not a private, cozy little ritual between you and God, but an encounter with Christ and others that opens you up to the world.

BOTH NOW AND IN THE FUTURE

So Christ melds his life with your life and the lives of others.
This brings about love encounters among him, you, and others,
not only during the liturgy but in the days that follow. But he
doesn't stop there. Gradually your life moves into the future,
toward ultimate union with Christ.

The ultimate future is the end of time, the final consumma-
tion, when Christ transforms the universe into the place of your
resurrected body. The Eucharist is a promise and a foretaste of
that future. Christ gathers all of your past in the present moment
and draws your life forward into the ultimate future. He enables
you to begin, even now, to experience your future reality. Don't
try to squeeze the Eucharist into some small box in your mind.
Leave yourself open—your feelings, your mind, your heart.

By now you may have noticed how several of the most important themes in this book converge and blend. The description
of encounter, love, God's inner life, your risen existence, and
the Mass event are all basically the same. Encounter in the full
sense—love, God's inner life, heaven, the Eucharist—is all of a
piece. If you have noticed this, it means you're beginning to get
it all together.

Our brief consideration of the three sacraments of initiation—Baptism, Confirmation, and Eucharist—has tried to point
up an aspect of our life in the church that can sometimes be
missed. Actions that may look to the detached observer like
mere conventional religious rituals are really mysterious realities
that can have a powerful impact on our lives. Only with the eyes
of faith can we see beneath the surface of these actions and
perceive the currents of interaction among Christ, ourselves, and
others. The world of the supernatural is like that: impervious to
the naked eye but nonetheless real.

The pouring of water, anointing with oil, eating and drinking
bread and wine seem like prosaic activities, but they are the
vehicles of Christ's loving encounters with us. Only when we
look beneath ceremonies to underlying events, only when we
look beyond immediate, palpable feelings to long-term, inner

transformation, will we begin to appreciate the riches that await us in the church's sacramental life.

Things to Do

1. Receiving the Eucharist is an intensely personal, *individual* experience. On the other hand, it also has important, far-reaching *social* dimensions. Explain how both of these characteristics are verified in Holy Communion.
2. It has been repeatedly stressed here that biblical narratives are not merely long-ago events past and gone, but events that we actually live in sacramental experiences. Explain how, in the Eucharist, we participate in the following biblical events:
   • The manna in the desert (Exodus 16)
   • The miracle of the loaves (John 6)
   • The Last Supper (Mark 14:12-25)
3. Bring in recent copies of your parish bulletin and your diocesan paper. What items suggest that the parish may be a community and not a fort?
4. People often complain, "I don't get anything out of Mass." What do they mean? Using the ideas expressed in this chapter, help them deal with this problem.

19

Going Public

When we decide that religion is not just another consumption item, we begin to take the Gospel seriously. When we think of Christianity not just as a series of doctrines, laws, and practices, and make it the basis of our vision, values, and commitments, then we are on the way to becoming not religious consumers but disciples of Christ. But how can we tell whether we have really caught the vision and put on the mind of Christ? How do we know when we, as individuals and as a church, are being faithful to the Good News?

Recall once again that passage in the Acts of the Apostles that describes the early church as it emerged at Pentecost. A careful reading of that group portrait of the first Christians offers us an excellent standard by which to judge the quality of our own discipleship. After Peter announces the news of the resurrection of Jesus from the dead, he calls upon his hearers to repent and be baptized and thus receive the Holy Spirit.

Those who accepted his message were baptized, and about three thousand persons were added that day. They devoted themselves to the teaching of the apostles and to the communal life, to the breaking of the bread and to the prayers.

Awe came upon everyone, and many wonders and signs were done through the apostles. All who believed were together and had all things in common; they would sell their property and possessions and divide them among all according to each one's need. Every day they devoted themselves to meeting together in the temple area and to breaking bread in their homes. They ate their meals with exultation and sincerity of heart, praising God and enjoying favor with all the people. And every day the Lord added to their number those who were being saved. — Acts 2:41-47

Who, then, were the Christians, and how could you tell? They were those who *accepted his message* and believed in Jesus Christ, God made human, dead, and risen for us. They were the *baptized,* who had been born again and received into the church. They *devoted themselves to the teaching of the apostles and to the communal life*; they never stopped learning, trying to come to a more mature faith as they took on more adult responsibilities. And they did this not in isolation but in *communal life,* ready to learn from one another.

The *breaking of the bread and the prayers* were at the heart of their life together. The Eucharist was the center of their worship, and they were a praying people. From the Eucharist and their prayer life there flowed *signs and wonders* — not just spectacular miracles but, more importantly, the day-by-day, down-to-earth loving deeds of caring and compassion and generosity without which life would be scarcely bearable.

Finally, they *sold their property and possessions and divided them among all according to each one's need.* They took responsibility for one another and let nothing stand in the way of providing for the needy. Their whole scale of values was rearranged, and their social order was transformed into one that cared for people above all else.

What does this group portrait tell us about how to live as Christians? That we who believe in Jesus Christ and have been baptized in his name are to be both hearers and doers of the word, striving as we grow older to know Christ better, to love him more, and to follow him more faithfully. That we must lead lives of prayer, and that the center of our prayer life is the Eucharist. That we must do "signs and wonders," confounding the cynics of this world by refusing to live by the law of the jungle. This means making our money honestly, sharing it unselfishly, refusing to make it an idol, and devoting our lives to goals more noble than material accumulation and conspicuous consumption. Finally, that we are to take responsibility for one another, especially for those in need. If there is such a thing as a checklist for judging our church's fidelity to God's call, this is it.

A NEW UNDERSTANDING

Our understanding of the last item on the checklist, taking responsibility for one another, has evolved in recent years the way the others have not. There is something constant and unchanging about announcing in every age the life, death, and resurrection of Christ, celebrating the Eucharist, and encouraging the faithful to good deeds of justice and love. But the injunction to care for one another is interpreted by more and more Christians today in ways that were scarcely thought of a few decades ago. Consider, for example, charity toward the poor. Christians, like members of other religions and those who practice philanthropy without any religious motivation, have always considered it a duty and a privilege to give help to those less fortunate. Jesus' parable of the rich man and Lazarus (Luke 16:19-31), and his description of the last judgment (Matthew 25:31-46), in which salvation depends on how one treated the neighbor, are part of a rich tradition that supports the concern that Jesus' followers have always had for the needy. This will always be an essential part of Christian life.

But today many are asking, *"why* are people poor?" The reasons are many, of course, and vary from person to person. Often the causes are beyond one's control, and then the poor person is a victim. But a victim of what? Bad luck? Suppose that the dice are loaded in such a way that some people are bound to lose, no matter how hard they try. Suppose the game is rigged so that they never had a chance to win. That sounds like a conspiracy. But conspiracies come in many shapes and sizes. Some are conscious plots entered into deliberately by dishonest and greedy people who contrive to get rich at the expense of the poor. In a just society, laws enacted for the common good should prevent or penalize such exploitation. But as anyone knows who wasn't born yesterday, the exploiters can often manipulate the laws to their own advantage. They can use their power and their wits to prevent any effective interference with their machinations. They are involved in corruption, but the corruption is legal, and that makes all the difference.

Those are conscious conspiracies. But they could rarely succeed if there were not unconscious conspiracies to pave the way. Unconscious conspiracy? Isn't that a contradiction? Not really. In a democratic state such as ours, the institutions and laws by which we live are considered the will of the people. In theory, we the citizens have the power, through our elected representatives, to enact and change laws, even to amend the nation's Constitution. That is why we call ourselves a free people. The economic, political, and social arrangements by which we live are not imposed on us by a tyrant but are perceived as the expression of our communal will. Of course, not all citizens agree with all the arrangements, but the majority rules. Those who dissent are obliged to abide by the will of the majority, even as they are permitted and encouraged to try by persuasion to convert the majority to their point of view.

So where is the unconscious conspiracy? Whenever institutions and laws that promote or fail to oppose injustice are left in place, either through citizen ignorance or apathy, then we are all implicated in the injustice, whether we realize it or not. These things are always easier to see in retrospect. When the founders of our country, in order to obtain ratification of the Constitution, compromised on the issue of slavery, they unwittingly created a monster that corrupted this nation for generations and whose bitter legacy still torments us today in a society torn by racial discord. Generations of Americans in the nineteenth century either supported or accepted the institution of slavery or decried it without feeling obliged to do away with it. The few who actively opposed it, the Abolitionists, were for the most part looked upon as radical activists and troublemakers.

Even after slavery was abolished, the next hundred years saw the perpetuation of *de jure* racial segregation. Many knew it was evil, but few felt obliged to oppose it until the civil rights movement of the sixties finally succeeded. The struggle of women to obtain the right to vote was a long and arduous one because so many fair-minded people remained on the sidelines. The intern-

ment of American citizens of Japanese descent on the Pacific
Coast after Pearl Harbor aroused almost no cries of protest.

LEARNING FROM THE PAST

All this is relatively ancient history, but there are lessons still
to be learned. All those arrangements—the institution of slavery, racial segregation, the denial of voting rights to women, and
the wartime internments—were all undeniably legal and just as
undeniably unjust. American citizens, whether they realized it
or not, were parties to conspiracies that systematically robbed
people of their basic human rights. Some were silent out of
ignorance, others out of apathy. Many were Christians who took
seriously the command of Jesus to love one another, but never
made the connection between that injunction and what was
going on all around them.

So the question arises: What is happening now? Are there
any unconscious conspiracies taking place at this moment, and
are we part of them? Is the free society of which we are members
functioning in ways that respect the dignity and rights of all, or
are there built-in mechanisms of injustice at work? Or put the
question another way. What are we doing—or failing to do—
today that our children will condemn us for twenty or thirty years
from now? We look back on the institutionalized injustices of a
generation or a century ago and wonder: Why did no one speak
out? Why were the churches silent? Where were the Christians
when their oppressed and neglected neighbors needed them?
Will future generations look back at us and pass the same judgment? How will we appear in their eyes? More to the point:
How do we appear in the eyes of God, the defender of the poor,
the widow, and the orphan?

In passing judgment on the actions or inaction of people in
the past, we must make allowances for the fact that they were
not as socially aware as we are. It would be unfair, as well as
anachronistic, for us to read into those times a level of moral
sophistication that simply was not there. But today we know
more, we are better informed, our consciousness has been
raised. We can no longer plead ignorance in the face of institutionalized evil. As Jesus says in another context, more will be

demanded of those to whom more has been given (Luke 12:48).

There are always religious people, including many Christians, who resist this line of thinking. They cannot think of economic, social, and political realities in religious terms. Slogans such as "keep religion out of politics" seem to absolve them from any active involvement in social change. They see religion as limited to the realm of the sacred, the spiritual, the eternal. They fear it will be corrupted by contamination with secular concerns. Here we recognize an old enemy, the false god of the status quo. The bishops of the Second Vatican Council were forthright in their rejection of this false god, and the false religion that goes with it, in the *Pastoral Constitution on the Church in the Modern World:*

This Council exhorts Christians, as citizens of two cities, to strive to discharge their earthly duties conscientiously and in response to the Gospel spirit. They are mistaken who, knowing that we have here no lasting city but seek one which is to come, think that they may therefore shirk their earthly responsibilities. For they are forgetting that by the faith itself they are more than ever obliged to measure up to those duties, each according to his proper vocation.

Nor, on the contrary, are they any less wide of the mark who think that religion consists in acts of worship alone and in the discharge of certain moral obligations, and who imagine that they can plunge themselves into earthly affairs in such a way as to imply that these are altogether divorced from the religious life. This split between the faith which many profess and their daily lives deserves to be counted among the more serious errors of our age. Long since, the prophets of the Old Testament fought vehemently against this scandal and even more so did Jesus Christ in the New Testament threaten it with grave punishments.

Therefore, while we are warned that it profits a man nothing if he gain the whole world and lose himself, the expectation of a new earth must not weaken but rather stimulate our concern for cultivating this one. For here grows the body ... which is able to give some foreshadowing of the new age.

Earthly progress must be carefully distinguished from the growth of Christ's kingdom. Nevertheless, to the extent that the former can contribute to the better ordering of human society, it is of vital concern to the kingdom of God (nn. 91-94, 76-77).

Several aspects of our national life make it difficult for us to accept this teaching wholeheartedly and follow through in practice. The popular slogan, "separation of church and state," which was originally intended to protect us from the imposition of a state religion, has been used to reduce religion to a purely private affair. In the interest of civil harmony and national unity, freedom *of* religion has become freedom *from* religion. Thus religion is seen as a purely private matter which should have no impact on public life. This is just another manifestation of religious individualism. But this time it not only discourages identification with community and tradition, but also encourages social irresponsibility.

The opposite error is reducing religion to a political or social service program. This is what people rightly resist when they view with suspicion the intrusion of religion into the public arena. But both extremes—the reduction of religion to secular programs and the exclusion of religion from all secular concerns—must be avoided. Otherwise we will continue to make the same tragic mistakes over and over again, sinning by silence in the face of social injustice. Christians must resist the privatization of religion, even as they respect the differences among people and refrain from imposing particular religious beliefs on those of other faiths. There is no other way to fulfill Jesus' command to love and care for one another. More than private charity, people need justice and care in the social realm, in the world of laws and contracts and jobs and public education. If we are really serious about loving and caring for our neighbor, we have to go beyond the world of private, one-on-one justice and charity and become involved in the wider world of social action.

FACING THE ISSUES

What would this involvement look like, in the concrete? What kind of social action is expected of the followers of Christ? Before we try to answer that, we must put a prior question. What should be the objects of our reflection? What are some of the issues that command our attention and concern?

A partial list would include such matters as the economy, defense spending, women's rights, abortion, and environmental concerns. There are many others, but these will suffice as examples.

The Economy

Jesus said that the poor would always be with us, but since the 1980s they seem to be with us in greater numbers than at any time since the Great Depression. We are appalled by the growing numbers of homeless people. The proportion of Americans living in poverty is a scandal. The extremes of inequality are profoundly disturbing. Something is radically wrong in a society which suffers from no lack of natural resources but is unable to provide the opportunity for a decent life to growing numbers of its citizens.

There are no simple answers to these questions, and we feel powerless in the face of seemingly intractable economic forces. Guilt and frustration await those who care. But we can at least inform ourselves of the issues, get at the facts, consider the suggested solutions. We must be convinced that our nation's economy, which tolerates and even promotes so much needless human suffering, is not the product of blind, inexorable forces, but the result of free decisions knowingly made by those who wield the power of wealth and influence. Too many citizens look upon economic institutions and practices as untouchable, beyond the reach of criticism or any moral judgment. There may be little that we can do about these enormous problems, but the way we vote, the way we do business, the way we choose careers may have some impact.

Defense Spending

There is a real connection between the problems just described and the proportion of our national resources that we devote to warmaking capability. As informed and thinking voters, we should try to contribute to the public debate about priorities. How much for guns, how much for butter? Can the volume of military expenditures be justified in a nation where millions sleep on the street and eat in soup kitchens? These are not idle questions, but matters of life and death.

Women's Rights

The feminist agenda has been in the forefront of the national consciousness for several years now. Good people can and do disagree about some of the demands put forward there. But we all have the duty to consider seriously those issues which touch on basic justice. In the past, women have been treated as second-class citizens. Discrimination against women goes back a long way and is deeply rooted in the history of our civilization. There is no longer any excuse for perpetuating or tolerating attitudes and practices which attribute to women anything less than full human dignity.

Abortion

In the minds of many of our fellow citizens, abortion comes under the heading of women's rights. We must do all we can, by education and example, to put this issue where it belongs. Millions of unborn human beings are being deprived of that most basic of all rights, the right to life. The quality of the debate about this life-and-death question is depressingly low. Earnest, well-meaning people are found on both sides of this question that divides the nation. We must try to get beyond slogans, to listen and speak to one another and do what we can to stop the killing.

Environmental Concerns

God gave us this earth and put us in charge. The evidence is overwhelming that we are doing a very bad job of caring for the planet. More and more people are becoming concerned and getting involved in efforts to save the only world we have. Ranged against them are deeply entrenched special interests, longstanding apathy, and genuine concern about the short-term negative effects of some efforts to preserve the environment. But to do nothing is to condemn later generations to suffer as a result of our neglect. Here is one of those questions that our children and grandchildren will ask: "Where were you when . . . ?"

These are just a few of the more pressing issues that demand our attention. They are only part of a worldwide net of intertwined crises. But they do force us to confront ourselves and ask how serious we are about loving and caring for our neighbor. They are all about justice and responsibility—about love in action. We are all on the road from Jerusalem to Jericho, and our neighbor lies stricken by the side of the road. Shall we pass by, like the priest and the Levite? Or shall we, like the Good Samaritan, do what has to be done? Maybe we can't do much. God does not ask the impossible. But we have to care, be ready to do whatever we can to make a difference, and support those who can do more. In any case, we are not alone. In the church, we can stand together in solidarity with the poor and the oppressed. And God's help is ready at hand.

Things to Do

1. What are today's unconscious conspiracies?
2. What will future generations criticize us for doing or failing to do?
3. Are we doing anything now that future generations will praise us for?
4. Are there other issues of social justice, besides those mentioned here, that Christians should address together?
5. Why is it so difficult to convince rank-and-file Catholics that action for justice is at the heart of the Gospel?

20

Who Is My Neighbor?

Once we begin to care about justice issues such as the ones mentioned at the end of the last chapter and ask what we can do about them, we have taken an important step in our faith life. Just thinking about such problems in terms of our response to the call of Christ is a breakthrough. We are now going beyond religious consumerism and moving toward discipleship. God's command to love our neighbor is no longer an abstraction but a specific call to work for justice in the concrete circumstances of the real world.

An important step, yes; but only a first step. As urgent and relevant as these issues are, they comprise a very limited list of those that demand our concern. Issues such as poverty, homelessness, women's rights, defense spending, abortion, and damage to the environment are unavoidable. They assault us daily and compel our attention. But they are only the large tip of a much larger iceberg. As domestic problems, they confront us in our roles as citizens of this country. To deal with them in isolation is to fall into a lesser form of parochialism. We shall begin to get a hold on them only when we begin to think in worldwide terms and see them as local manifestations of a much larger web of structural evil. Living in a global village demands global thinking if we are to deal effectively with the forces that undermine our societies and poison our way of life. Some of these forces are so pervasive and so deeply entrenched that a new kind of thinking is needed in order to extirpate them. We must get beyond symptoms and address the underlying causes and processes that generate and perpetuate injustice.

Many of these causes and processes are located within political, economic, social, and religious systems based on power and submission. Those who have the power exercise it unilaterally and force the rest to submit. The power monopoly is often exercised by an oligarchy, while individuals have to submit just to survive. If they refuse to submit, they are branded as nonpersons.

As long as all power flows from the top, those who exercise it are free to construct and maintain systematic patterns of injustice. As long as these systems are seen as above criticism, it is impossible to get at the real issue. But since the systems are sanctioned by law, those who challenge them are branded as lawless. Thus law itself, whose proper function in a just society is to protect the rights of the powerless and promote the common good, is corrupted at its roots, for those in power use it to preserve the status quo and perpetuate a system that rewards the unscrupulous few. That same system not only punishes the rest but also condemns them as criminals if they criticize the process of oppression.

In a world of unjust systems, we have to find out who wields unjust power and challenge them. We must alert the unwitting functionaries who uncritically serve the system. And we must empower the victims who, all too often, have failed to question the system and hence accepted their condition as inevitable.

It doesn't take a great deal of imagination to fill in this picture with the names and details of institutions and societies past and present. (It may take more insight and self-knowledge to recognize these processes at work in institutions closer to home.) We all know of countries where extremes of obscene wealth and grinding poverty coexist, where the gap between them grows ever wider. In such societies, where hopelessness and despair are the order of the day for all but a privileged few, economic conditions are inextricably intertwined with the political processes that ensure the protection of privilege. The forces of law and order are committed to the maintenance of the status quo and inevitably end up brutalizing the victims of the social order. The media of public information become organs of propaganda dedicated to discrediting all dissent, outlawing those who question the prevailing system, and convincing the populace that things were meant to be this way and could never be any different.

These pictures are depressing enough, but they become even more disturbing when we are told that we may be implicated in the horrors perpetrated by these regimes. We know that multinationals based in the United States are deeply involved in the economic structures just described. For decades during the late, unlamented Cold War, our government consistently propped up and supported right-wing dictatorships in our frantic vendetta against the forces (real and imagined) of communism. Our leaders told us that we were fighting for justice against tyranny, and many of us believed them. Some of us still do. It is time at least to question such claims, to make sure that we are not the unwitting accomplices of injustice and oppression on a grand scale. And we have a serious obligation to examine whether our own society's economic well-being, limited as it is, is being purchased at the expense of human suffering elsewhere through the manipulation of economic forces worldwide.

In these dysfunctional societies, where injustice and oppression are built into their very way of life, the church tries to carry on the work of Jesus Christ. In some places, church leaders and members oppose the status quo and work for social, economic, and political change. In others, they go along with systemic evil in order to get along. Sometimes church leaders and members find themselves in opposing camps, some supporting the system and others denouncing it. Finally, some try to be neutral and to stay above the battle. But in doing so they actually support the status quo which is so firmly established that only a determined people can effect meaningful change.

THE ROOTS OF PASSIVITY

How is it that different groups of Christians can respond so differently to this kind of challenge? The reasons will differ from place to place, from group to group, from person to person. But some factors seem fairly clear. Sometimes the structures of church groups themselves promote passivity. Power is concentrated exclusively in the leadership instead of being shared. Participation in decision making is discouraged. Unquestioning obedience is esteemed and rewarded. Questioning and critical thinking are not only not promoted but are even seen as betrayal. Church members are starkly divided into commanders and obeyers, teachers and learners, rule makers and rule observers, with no room for input and dialogue. This is the kind of ecclesiastical structure that promotes what we earlier called traditional faith — a willing submission to indoctrination, keeping in step, following directions, accepting without question both the goals of the group and the approved means of achieving them. Individuality is sacrificed to conformity, security is bought at the price of responsibility, and no one may march to any but the official drummer.

By and large, church members who operate at this traditional faith level are good people who are trying to be better. They take their faith seriously and, within their limited vision, try to live up to it. If church leaders were always wise and without faults, and if church structures always promoted and supported what was best in people, then theoretically there would be no problem with members remaining at the traditional or "parade" level.

But of course, as Jesus himself foresaw, this is a church of sinners, with flawed people and flawed procedures. It is inevitable that from time to time leaders will lead unwisely, teach less than adequately, and manipulate and treat unjustly those under them. When injustice occurs in the making and enforcing of church laws and practices, the church fails to practice what is preached. That is bad enough. But what is even worse is that a church which encourages and even tries to impose a "parade" mentality creates people who uncritically support the status quo not only in the church but also in the political, economic, and social order of their civil society. There is a tragic irony here. The very institution which calls on people to take a prophetic stance on justice clings to structures that prevent people from taking a prophetic stance.

Do not misunderstand. We are not saying that church members operating at traditional levels of faith are incapable of responding to moral demands arising from unjust structures. They can and do respond with compassion and generosity to human suffering and need. They reach out to the victims of oppression, bind up their wounds, and gladly make sacrifices in order to improve their lot. But they respond only to symptoms. They are incapable of taking that one further, crucial step and criticizing the systems which, if left in place, are guaranteed to perpetuate the very conditions that evoke their sympathy.

It takes not only critical insight but also a great deal of psychological courage to go beyond symptoms and question systems. This is true in all the significant areas of life — political, economic, social, and religious. Civil and religious institutions provide us with what we all want to believe is an orderly and predictable world that consistently responds with justice and care to legitimate human aspirations. For fair-minded, law-abiding people, it is profoundly unsettling even to suspect that the ordinary machinery of our civil and religious life is not only not defending the rights of people but may actually be systematically undermining them. That is why, as we pointed out above, it is difficult to question systems as well as symptoms, even of distant societies, but even more difficult in those closer to home.

Most of us do not like to think of ourselves as radicals, which is a pejorative term in most circles. But the word comes from the Latin *radix*, the word for "root." Dealing with symptoms and ignoring systemic evil is like trying to remove weeds with a lawn mower. You have to get down deeper and pull them out by the roots. Removing weeds from your lawn this way can give you a sore back. Trying to remove the roots of social injustice can get you in big trouble, not only with the people in power, but even with those who ought to be on your side but are frightened by radicals. But that is part of the cost of discipleship.

There is an understandable but misguided reluctance on the part of church ministers to engage in serious critical examination of church structures. As we have pointed out elsewhere (*Integral Justice*, p. 79):

In justice ministry, some ministers, as they hear the cries of those oppressed by political, economic, and social unjust systems, are tempted to ignore the fourth system, the ecclesiastical component. "Let's not dissipate our energies. Let's not get involved (although fully justified to do so) with in-house matters. Let's 'bite the bullet' so that we can serve the victims of political, economic, and social injustice."

This is a misreading of the signs of the times. If ecclesiastical injustice is ignored, a number of the present mechanisms of church structure stay in place. These mechanisms are geared to keep people at the socialization level of faith appropriation. We have seen that people at this level have a psychological bias against evaluating any political, economic, social, or religious system. Therefore, they cannot hear (or respond to) the challenge of church teaching on political, economic, or social systemic injustice. If the fourth component of justice (religious) is not practiced, the other three are doomed to failure.

WHAT IS AT STAKE

What will be the price of failure to engage in criticism and reform of systems and structures? Obviously, the continuation of economic, social, and political injustice. We, the church, will have failed in our prophetic duty to influence the world around us. Past sins of omission, like the failure to condemn slavery and racial segregation, will be repeated. We will once again leave untouched the roots of oppression in society. That is bad enough, but it is not all. Religion itself runs the risk not only of being ineffective, but of even being corrupted at its core, as a group of Third World Christians point out in *The Road to Damascus* (p. 15):

Throughout history, we Christians have often been deaf to God's voice and blind to God's presence in people. This lack of faith has prevented us from exercising the prophetic mission that Jesus has given us. We have often been silent instead of denouncing injustice and oppression. Instead of working for justice and liberation, we have often remained uninvolved.

How shall we explain this silence and uninvolvement, this blindness and unbelief? For some of us, the reason lies in a life that is not confronted by the suffering and struggle of the poor, and therefore the choice of a convenient God who does not challenge us to take part in a movement for change. For others, however, the reason lies in a choice of privilege and power, and a *conscious* defence of the status quo. In many cases, it includes taking part in attacks against movements for change, in repression and the killing of the poor.

For such people, it is not simply an inability to see and hear; it is a refusal to see and hear. It is not merely lack of faith in the God of life; it is the worship of a false god — the sin of idolatry.

We referred above to those countries where church members, both leaders and followers, are split into opposing camps, some supporting the status quo and others denouncing it. Their disagreement is not just about economics and politics. Those who knowingly support manifestly unjust regimes and yet claim to be Christian strike at the very heart of our faith. In the name of God they stand for what God rejects. Theirs is the sin of hypocrisy, the sin that is most passionately denounced by Jesus in the Gospels. He condemned the religious leaders of his day for using their position and influence to mislead the people. The same thing is going on here.

In many places in the world today, there are two new competing versions of Christianity that cut across sectarian lines. Each has its own image of God and Jesus, its own reading of the Gospel, and its own leaders and followers. These two versions are irreconcilable. In some developing countries and police states, the differences are stark and unmistakable, and people feel called upon to choose between them. In others, the issues are not as clear-cut. The idols here may be consumerism or materialism or some other false god that promises total security at the price of unconditional loyalty. One is reminded of H. Richard Niebuhr's devastating description of what he called the pseudogospel: A God without wrath brought people without sin into a kingdom without judgment through the ministrations of a Christ without a cross. Whatever the idols are, they conspire to rob their worshipers of any sense of urgency in the quest for justice. They offer convenient rationalizations for all sorts of compromises and betrayals, and gradually make them deaf to the cries of the poor and impervious to any appeal to conscience.

Some are blind by choice, but not all. Many uncritical defenders of unjust systems have a limited, distorted image of God and understanding of religion. As we pointed out earlier, many people think of God as concerned only with certain aspects of reality — the spiritual, the eternal, the sacred. The rest of life — the material, the earthly, the secular — has no intrinsic value. Religion then is about the soul, about heaven, about prayer and worship. To bring into the sanctuary such "worldly" matters as economic and political concerns is to debase religion instead of keeping it pure and unsullied. This is a world-denying faith, an ideology that distorts Christianity not by stressing the spiritual and the sacred but by devaluing the earthly, day-to-day concerns that occupy us here and now in this vale of tears.

It is obvious that this pseudofaith is tailor-made for those who want to think of themselves as Christians even though their values and priorities and commitments blatantly contradict the teaching of Christ. This contradiction has been pointed out explicitly by the fathers of the Second Vatican Council.

This kind of dualism has been around for a long time, and tends to turn up in one form or another at least every few centuries. In times of oppression it can serve both the oppressors and the oppressed. The former use it to insulate themselves from social concern, and the latter find refuge in an escapist religion that offers comfort in the promise of a better world in the hereafter. It can be used to discredit reformers by depicting them as disturbers of the peace, rebels against God's will, and corrupters of religion. They thus project onto their adversaries their own antisocial bias. This sort of thing has been happening to prophets long before Jesus appeared on the scene:

> I hate, I spurn your feasts,
>   I take no pleasure in your solemnities;
> Your cereal offerings I will not accept,
>   nor consider your stall-fed peace offerings.
> Away with your noisy songs!
>   I will not listen to the melodies of your harps.
> But if you would offer me holocausts,

> then let justice surge like water,
> and goodness like an unfailing stream.
> —Amos 5:21-24

Woe to you, scribes and Pharisees, you hypocrites. You build the tombs of the prophets and adorn the memorials of the righteous, and you say, "If we had lived in the days of our ancestors, we would not have joined them in shedding the prophets' blood." Therefore, behold, I send to you prophets and wise men and scribes; some of them you will kill and crucify, some of them you will scourge in your synagogues and pursue from town to town, so that there may come upon you all the righteous blood shed on earth, from the righteous blood of Abel to the blood of Zechariah, the son of Barachiah, whom you murdered between the sanctuary and the altar.

Jerusalem, Jerusalem, you who kill the prophets and stone those sent to you, how many times I yearned to gather your children together, as a hen gathers her young under her wings, but you were unwilling! —Matthew 23:29-30, 34-35, 37

WHO IS MY NEIGHBOR?

This can all be somewhat intimidating. Does being a Christian really involve all this? Is discipleship this demanding? Are we making Jesus' simple message more complicated than it really is?

The best way to find out is to ask Jesus himself. When the lawyer asked him what it was all about, he was told to love God with all his heart and his neighbor as himself. When he asked, "Who is my neighbor?" Jesus replied with the story of the Good Samaritan. As we pointed out in *Do the Right Thing* (pp. 4-5):

What is Jesus saying to you and me in this story? It is clear that by "love of neighbor" he is not talking about a vague feeling of good will or just "being nice." He's talking about *action*. If someone needs me, I'm supposed to *do* something ... Love of God and neighbor means more than warm feelings, more than avoiding the breaking of rules. It means living up to the responsibility we normally feel toward those who are closest to us, and extending that love to all of God's children without exception. That's a big order! To do this, we have to stop thinking of people in terms of "us" and "them." If we are serious about following Christ, we must try to stop dividing people up into two groups, those we should care about and those who don't matter.

So if I want to be a disciple of Christ, I cannot settle for just minding my own business. In answer to Cain's question, yes, I am my brother's and sister's keeper. In the world view of Jesus and his followers, there are no strangers, only brothers and sisters, for we are all children of God. We are challenged to put aside all tribalism and see all persons as members of our family. All of them have a call on my concern, especially those in need. The poor must have a special place in my heart, as they did in Christ's.

Who are these poor? Not only the materially poor, the homeless and the hungry, but also the spiritually deprived, those who have been denied freedom, self-determination, a sense of worth, or dignity. There may be very little I can do for them, but I am ready and willing to do what I can. In solidarity with other members of the church, I am ready to help mobilize our resources to make a better world.

Today we disciples of Christ understand, better than previous generations, what is involved in effective love of the neighbor, in responding to the real needs of real people. We are no longer content to deal with symptoms, we are ready to confront systems. Refusing to restrict religion to the private sphere, we reject political apathy in the face of institutionalized evil. Responding to the bishops who have declared justice to be a constitutive dimension of the Gospel, we are committed to world justice. In pursuing this goal, we identify with the needy and the outcast and exercise a preferential option for the poor. We see these duties not just as personal obligations, but as a calling addressed to the whole church together, the people of God.

We believe that in pursuing these goals we are correctly reading the signs of the times and responding to God's revelation in history. We hope thereby to put love where it belongs, at the center of the church's social teaching, and that this love is best expressed today in the pursuit of justice for all. This means more than making statements and passing resolutions. It means reflecting together on our experience, talking action, and reflecting prayerfully on the appropriateness and the effectiveness of that action.

All of this we do in the conviction that we are all one human family, with mutual obligations to promote the rights and development of all people across the world. This means that rich nations have the duty to assist poor nations, so that international structures and order may be truly just.

> Then the king will say to those on his right, "Come, you who are blessed by my Father. Inherit the kingdom prepared for you from the foundation of the world. For I was hungry and you gave me food, I was thirsty and you gave me drink, a stranger and you welcomed me, naked and you clothed me, ill and you cared for me, in prison and you visited me. Amen, I say to you, whatever you did for one of these least brothers of mine, you did for me." —Matthew 25:34-36, 40

Things to Do

1. Do you think that this country shares responsibility for poverty elsewhere in the world?
2. Have your experiences in church helped you to move beyond the traditional level of faith?
3. Have you ever been involved, or seen others involved, in challenging structural injustice?
4. What did holiness mean to you in the past? Has your understanding changed?
5. Do you think that escapist, dualistic religion is enduring or fading away?
6. What can we do, here and now, to begin to achieve these goals?

Epilogue

This book began with cries of the heart. We felt at one with all the men and women who search for some greater meaning in their lives, some sense of enduring significance in the joys and sorrows and achievements and failures that make up their life stories. We recognized this quest for fulfillment as the religious impulse which, from time to time, moves nearly everyone to try to make larger sense of their lives.

When we gave this impulse free rein and a name, we got beneath the conventional, often misleading ideas of religion. At its most authentic, religion is the attempt to encounter God and others and thus fulfill the deepest longings of our hearts. There followed a search for the real God, clearing away the underbrush of inadequate and distorted images. Presently the God revealed in Jesus Christ emerged: One who is intimately involved in our lives, engaged in sponsoring the process of evolution, and inviting us to join in as co-evolvers of the universe.

This God calls us to encounter and work with others in community. This means relating to others as persons, dealing with the challenges and frustrations that accompany all serious attempts to get along with the rest of the world. We learned that the yardstick whereby we can judge the condition of our relationship to God is the quality of our relationships with other human beings. We are actually expected to love them—*all* of them!—even the stranger and the enemy. We are supposed to expand the horizons of our caring ever outward, embracing without exception the whole human race. The key to this achievement, which in purely human terms is impossible, is the realization that in a world where all are daughters and sons of God, there are no strangers, only family. In families, animosities are understandable, but enmity is unthinkable. The law of love knows no bounds.

All this is easy to say but much harder to do. Unaided, human powers are unequal to the task. So God took the initiative and pitched camp among us in the person of Jesus of Nazareth. He took on all the demons that beset us, and a few more. He challenged the entrenched forces of self-interest, was apparently vanquished by them on the cross, but emerged triumphant in the Resurrection. This triumph is ours as well as his, for he lives on in us, the church, which is his body. He makes available to us the fullness of life in word and sacrament. These empower us to love him and others more deeply and so to commit ourselves to action for justice not only with regard to political, economic, and social systems, but also in religious structures. The greatest encounters center in the Eucharist, where the trans-geographical, transtemporal, transsocial Christ brings about meetings with those who are in need of action for justice and peace. If nothing else can do it, these Eucharistic encounters should convince us that such action is not an optional extra on the periphery of Christianity but lies at the very heart of the following of Christ.

Once we catch this vision and open ourselves to God's grace, all kinds of possibilities open up. We are now people persons, messengers of Christ's life to others. We can be prophets, helping to fulfill the prophetic role of the church. The love affair between us and God overflows to others in many ways. We become celebrants, giving voice to the love, joy, longings, and aspirations of others. As consolers, we comfort those who feel the heavy hand of failure, sickness, and death. As healers, we are extensions of Christ the healer. As disturbers, we remind the church and the world that we must evolve or perish. We become heralds, helping those caught in a critical boredom with life to surface and expand their heart wishes. We are visionaries, caught up in the joy of a universe evolving toward Christ, and spreading this joy to others. And in doing this we help to establish the reign of God in our world, providing a foretaste of the ultimate transformation of that world into a kingdom of justice, love, and peace.

When will you know if all these wonderful things have happened? Probably not right away. We hope that even now, after reading this book by yourself or with others, you have experienced the beginnings of this growth in Christ's life. But the most important and lasting effects of this journey we have taken together will probably surface later on. You have been trying to get in touch with the deepest part of yourself, to reach out to others in perhaps new and unfamiliar ways, and to surface and expand your most profound hopes and aspirations. Such enterprises take time. You cannot program encounters with the Holy Spirit any more than you can program falling in love. You can only prepare the soil and wait. Sometime in the near or distant future, the seeds sown now will bloom, and you will be surprised at how much was happening just beneath the surface of your life.

Perhaps you began this book looking for what we call in-love. This is the love that takes place in your personal life, within your family, in your community. There is a paradox here. The love within a group can grow just so much, and then it tends to stagnate unless it turns into out-love. When people get beyond the boundaries of their groups and widen their circle of concern, a surprise awaits them: The turning of their love outward brings on growth in the love life of the group. And this, in turn, feeds the out-love, in a spiral effect.

When you were being urged to turn outward, to hunger and thirst for social justice, to critique immoral systems on behalf of God's voiceless victims of injustice, you were being called to out-love. When the needy, the victimized, and the oppressed of the world become the focus of the life of your community, the in-love of that community will grow in ways that you could never have foreseen.

Beloved, let us love one another, because love is of God; everyone who loves is begotten by God and knows God. Whoever is without love does not know God, for God is love. In this way the love of God was revealed to us: God sent his only Son into the world so that we might have life through him. In this is love: not that we have loved God, but that he loved us and sent his Son as expiation for our sins. Beloved, if God so loved us, we also must love one another. No one has ever seen God. Yet, if we love one another, God remains in us, and his love is brought to perfection in us.

This is how we know that we remain in him and he in us, that he has given us of his Spirit. Moreover, we have seen and testify that the Father sent his Son as savior of the world. Whoever acknowledges that Jesus is the Son of God, God remains in him and he in God. We have come to know and to believe in the love God has for us.

God is love, and whoever remains in love remains in God and God in him. In this is love brought to perfection among us, that we have confidence on the day of judgment because as he is, so are we in this world. There is no fear in love, but perfect love drives out fear because fear has to do with punishment, and so one who fears is not yet perfect in love. We love because he first loved us. — 1 John 4:7-19

And so, not the end, but rather the beginning.

Bibliography

Bellah, Robert, et al. *Habits of the Heart.* New York: Harper & Row, 1985.

Briggs, Kenneth. "Religious Feeling Seen Strong in U.S." New York *Times,* December 9, 1984.

DiGiacomo, James. *Do the Right Thing.* Kansas City: Sheed & Ward, 1991.

Fowler, James. *Stages of Faith.* New York: Harper & Row, 1981.

Gross, Francis. *Introducing Erik Erikson.* Lanham, Md.: United Press of America, 1987.

Johnson, George Sim. "Everything Goes, Nothing Matters." IMAGE, February 3, 1991.

Kilbourne, Jean. "Still Killing Us Softly." Cambridge, Mass.: Cambridge Documentary Films.

Land, Philip. "A Shifting Social Approach," in Henriot et al., *Catholic Social Teaching: Our Best Kept Secret.* Maryknoll, N.Y.: Orbis Books, 1988; revised edition 1992.

Third World Christians. *The Road to Damascus: Kairos and Conversion.* Washington, D.C.: Center of Concern, 1989.

Walsh, John. *Integral Justice: Changing People Changing Structures.* Maryknoll, N.Y.: Orbis Books, 1990.

Walsh, John, and James DiGiacomo. *So You Want to Do Ministry.* Kansas City: Sheed & Ward, 1986.

Westerhoff, John. "Celebrating and Living the Eucharist: A Cultural Analysis." *Alternative Futures for Worship,* vol. 3. Collegeville, Minn.: Liturgical Press, 1987.